www.TheFreshDiet.com

Chef Yos

A FRESH TAKE ON DIETS

99 recipes from The Fresh Diet kitchens
that will please your palate and your waistline

Chef Yos Schwartz

Executive Chef of The Fresh Diet,
America's Premier Diet Meal-Delivery Program

Art Direction:
José Bila Rodríguez

Design:
José Bila Rodríguez, Bill Greaves

Production Manager:
Alejandro Perez-Eguren

Photography:
Stephen Flint Photography

Prop Stylist:
Tish Cindric

ISBN: 978-0-9849019-0-6

Printed in the United States of America
First printing: 2011   **www.TheFreshDiet.com   1-866-FRESH-50**

The Fresh Diet, Inc. 9429 Harding Ave #34 Surfside, FL 33154

Contents

FIND YOUR RECIPES IN A FLASH ─────────────────────────────

Always on a mission to make healthy eating as convenient as possible, we've sim-
plified the process of paging through all the recipes to find vegetarian or gluten-
free options. We've also included our own "favorites" icon to let you know which
recipes really got the crowds cheering. So if you're in a rush, if you have a particular
diet, or if you just want to know that you can find what you're looking for in a flash,
these icons are here to help you.

 Vegetarian   Gluten-Free   Favorite

About The Fresh Diet

At The Fresh Diet, every dish is created from a sincere passion for health, wellness and fresh ingredients. Since November 2005, The Fresh Diet has been providing our members with superior quality food and a successful weight loss program. Our plan is based on the recommended nutritionals of 30% lean protein, 40% good carbohydrates and 30% good fats. We eliminate the hard work of dieting by doing all of the weighing, measuring and preparing for you. What we leave for our clients is only an instruction to enjoy, savor and appreciate every meal and snack that they receive.

The Fresh Diet was the first diet-delivery company in Florida to offer clients fresh daily prepared meals that are never frozen, freeze-dried or vacuum-packed. Having experienced massive growth over the last five years, today our kitchens serve thousands of satisfied customers across the country every single day. Clients receive our three freshly prepared, delicious meals and two snacks delivered right to their door. Our mantra is fresh! We have never subscribed to the idea that a diet means deprivation. We firmly believe that by making use of the freshest ingredients, healthy food can have mouth-watering, delicious flavors.

The beauty of our program – aside from the convenience, weight loss and great taste that our clients love – is that our meals act as a teaching manual for a long-term healthy lifestyle. With a focus on FRESH ingredients, superb taste and healthy alternatives, The Fresh Diet is your answer.

Starting Fresh

Five hundred dollars on a credit card. Five customers in the greater Miami area. A belief, backed with research, that there was a huge market for a diet delivery service of fresh meals, prepared every day. That's how The Fresh Diet started in 2005, delivering customers three meals and two snacks a day. Six years later, we're serving 33 percent of the U.S. market, with plans to reach 98 percent of the country through mail delivery by the end of summer 2012.

My business partners and I are proud of what we've achieved, but here's what gives me the greatest satisfaction:

Two years ago, as the recession took hold in America, The Fresh Diet had grown to include the New York and Chicago markets, along with our existing foothold in Miami. We had just nine employees. Today when I turn on the news, I see all these stories about high unemployment numbers and companies cutting jobs. But our company has had the opposite experience. The Fresh Diet ended up growing so much, moving into markets such as California, Dallas, Houston, Washington DC, Philadelphia, Boston and even Toronto, that we now have 300 employees on our payroll.

I often wonder if we hadn't decided to start The Fresh Diet, where these employees would be. How would they be supporting their families? Knowing that we've been able to keep good people employed through some tough economic times has been incredibly rewarding to me.

It's not just our talented employees that make The Fresh Diet such a success in the highly competitive diet delivery market. We're also innovators. While our competitors send out meals that are frozen, freeze-dried or vacuum-packed, our customers get mouth-watering gourmet dishes. They're all carefully prepared by professional chefs in one of our corporate kitchens. Our customers also enjoy hands-on control over their daily meals and snacks by using our online meal planner.

A customer can't eat shellfish? No problem. Instead of choosing Crab Cakes Drizzled with Zesty Chipotle Lime Sauce, there are alternatives such as the Roasted Pork Loin with Apricot Curry Sauce (pg. 96). Our customers also have access to our registered dieticians, who can help them make the right choices, whether they're trying to lose a few pounds or fuel an activity-packed lifestyle.

As we move toward our second decade in business, we're designing exciting new programs for our customers. We're harnessing social media and technology in cool, innovative ways to build a community around our brand, and to help customers reach and maintain their health goals.

I have a vision that someday, when Fresh Diet customers stand on the scale in the morning, their weight will automatically upload into their personal profiles via Wi-Fi. Ideally we'll keep up with the latest kinds of health data so we can track our customers' nutritional needs.

This is great time for The Fresh Diet, and I'm so pleased that my best friend and our executive chef, Yosef Schwartz, has written this cookbook to share all that's good and delicious about The Fresh Diet. Fresh food that's simply prepared translates into recipes that are easy to follow and deliver tasty results.

Our goal is to bring our customers the freshest, most delicious meals possible. My wish for you: Eat well and thrive!

Zalmi Duchman
Chief Executive Officer, The Fresh Diet

Eating Well

For me, the passion for food began as an act of necessity. As a 13-year old student sent away to boarding school, I met my lifelong friend Zalmi and we quickly discovered that the food served in the school's cafeteria was just too terrible to endure. So I began to cook for the two of us. At first, I cooked up pastas and rice on a hot plate in my room, experimenting with herbs and spices to add more flavor. But before long, I was granted permission to use the school's own kitchen, creating larger meals for me and my friends.

This was the beginning of my own culinary journey, one that took me across the globe. From my training at Le Cordon Bleu College of Culinary Arts, to working in the kitchens of some of the most famous chefs in the world; what I learned, above all else, is that the best meals are based on using only the freshest ingredients.

And that's what The Fresh Diet is all about. When Zalmi and I started building this company six years ago, our mission was to bring healthy meals to our clients' doorsteps—meals that had been prepared with the best ingredients, cooked to the proper temperatures and consistencies, and delivered fresh.

That mission hasn't changed, and today we're constantly in the kitchen, testing new recipes and creating more options for our customers that adhere to a healthy balance of whole grains, protein, fruits and vegetables. Even as we've expanded our reach, I'm on the road to personally train each and every chef in all of our markets, making sure that they conform to our high standards.

Eating well is eating fresh, so there is nothing better than a home-cooked meal. That's why I'm sharing 99 of my favorite recipes from The Fresh Diet with you. They're all easy to prepare and use ingredients you can find at your local supermarket.

Fresh ingredients, simply prepared. That's our philosophy at The Fresh Diet, and we're delighted to be able to pass it along to you.

To your health!

Chef Yos Schwartz
Chief Culinary Officer, The Fresh Diet

The Well-Stocked Kitchen

When you have a few essential ingredients stocked in your cupboard and refrigerator, along with the right cooking tools in your kitchen, eating The Fresh Diet way is a breeze. The ingredients listed here are frequently used in Fresh Diet recipes. When you're ready to cook, just shop for the fresh ingredients required.

In the Pantry

Canned whole tomatoes
Canned beans: chickpeas, pinto beans
    and black beans
Fresh garlic
Yellow onions
Extra virgin olive oil
Cooking spray
Vegetable oil
Brown rice, medium grain
Quick-cook oatmeal
Cornstarch
Bittersweet chocolate chips
All-purpose flour
Baking soda
Baking powder
Light brown sugar
Canned water-packed tuna
Reduced-sodium chicken broth
Splenda, calorie-free sweetener,
    granulated honey
Reduced-sodium soy sauce
Corn flake crumbs
Balsamic vinegar
Fat-free mayonnaise

In the Refrigerator/Freezer

Reduced-fat milk
Reduced-fat plain yogurt
Part-skim ricotta cheese
Reduced-fat cream cheese
Reduced-fat sour cream
Eggs, large
Smart Balance® Buttery Spread
Parmigiano-Reggiano cheese (This is the real
    Parmesan cheese with its authentic
    designation marked on its rind.
    Avoid the pre-grated stuff in a can.)
Pre-washed, bagged salad mixes
Maple syrup (Once pure maple syrup is
    opened, it should be stored in the refrigerator.)
Lemons and limes
Bags of unsweetened frozen fruits

Kitchen Tools

3-quart saucepan with lid
8-inch chef's knife (Look for a knife that
    feels comfortable in your hand.)
Nonstick sauté pans (Nonstick pans usually don't
    last a lifetime, so there's no need to spend
    a fortune on the best. A department store pan
    with some heft will do.)
Silicone spatula
Metal spatulas
A variety of wooden or plastic cutting boards
    (Avoid glass, which dulls knives.)
Microplane® Zester
A variety of small, medium and
    large mixing bowls
Metal baking sheets (2)
Parchment paper
Liquid and solid measuring cups
    (From 1/4 to 1 cup measurements.)
Metal measuring spoons from 1/8 to
    1 tablespoon measurements
Meat thermometer (We like the digital thermometers
    that can be set to alarm when a certain internal
    temperature is reached.)
Kitchen timer
8- to 10-cup food processor (Here, you can spend
    several hundred dollars for all the bells and
    whistles, but a $50 model will handle most
    chopping, shredding and mixing jobs.)

Nice, but not Essential

Electric rice cooker (Makes cooking rice and
    grains a fuss-free experience.)
Knife sharpener (If you don't know how to use one,
    send your knives out for professional sharpening.)
Heavy-duty blender (Brands like Blendtec® and
    Vitamix® can run up to $500 or more but their
    motors are powerful and you'll have a blender
    that will last for years.)
Silpat® Non-Stick Silicone Baking Liner
    (Eliminates the need to grease a sheet pan.)
Garlic press (Essential if you cook with a lot of
    minced garlic. We like the handheld presses
    from OXO Good Grips™.)
Salad spinner
Electronic kitchen scale

BREAKFAST

RECIPES TO START YOUR DAY RIGHT.

Coconut Cream & Walnut Oatmeal

NUTRITIONAL INFORMATION
Per Serving

Calories:	319
Total Fat:	21 g
Cholesterol:	10 mg
Sodium:	356 mg
Total Carbohydrates:	27 g
Fiber:	3 g
Sugars:	7 g
Protein:	10 g

A warm bowl of oatmeal can be the perfect start to a cold wintery day — or if you're like us at The Fresh Diet, you can eat oatmeal all year long! Some people like their oatmeal chunky; others prefer it smooth. If you're in the latter camp, blend the cooked oatmeal with a hand-held immersion blender for 30 seconds before serving.

Look for canned cream of coconut in the Latin food section of your local grocer; we like the Coco Lopez® brand.

INGREDIENTS
1/3 c. quick oats
1/2 c. 2% milk
1/4 c. canned cream of coconut
1 tbsp. chopped walnuts
Salt to taste

DIRECTIONS
In small saucepan set over medium-low heat, combine all ingredients and bring to boil for 1 minute. Then, remove pan from heat and serve.

Prep time:	1 min.
Cook time:	1 min.
Total time:	2 min.
Yield:	1 serving
Serving size:	1 bowl

TOTAL TIME 2 min.

TOTAL TIME 2 min.

Toasted Granola with Diced Pears
& Honey Almond Ricotta Cheese

We love granola, so we created a delicious new dish with a flavorful ricotta cheese topping and chopped fresh pears that blend nicely with the granola's dried fruit.

Look for granola that's low in saturated fat, higher in polyunsaturated fats, and contains less that 10 g of sugar per serving.

INGREDIENTS

1/4 c. part-skim ricotta cheese

1 tsp. honey

1 tsp. chopped almonds

1/8 tsp. pure almond extract

1/2 c. granola

1/4 c. chopped fresh pear
   (approx. 1/3 pear)

DIRECTIONS

In small bowl, stir ricotta cheese, honey, chopped almonds and almond extract together. Transfer to a small serving bowl, and top with granola and pears.

Prep time:	2 min.
Cook time:	0 min.
Total time:	2 min.
Yield:	1 serving
Serving size::	1 bowl

NUTRITIONAL INFORMATION
Per Serving

Calories:	319
Total Fat:	21 g
Cholesterol:	10 mg
Sodium:	356 mg
Total Carbohydrates:	27 g
Fiber	3 g
Sugars:	7 g
Protein:	10 g

Southwestern-Style Scrambled Eggs with 9-Grain Toast

NUTRITIONAL INFORMATION
Per Serving

Calories:	294
Total Fat:	17 g
Cholesterol:	383 mg
Sodium:	705 mg
Total Carbohydrates:	18 g
Fiber:	1 g
Sugars:	4 g
Protein:	18 g

For Mexican food lovers, this breakfast is for you! You can control the level of heat in this recipe by choosing a mild (or spicy) salsa, or substituting regular Monterey Jack cheese for pepper jack.

INGREDIENTS

1/2 tsp. vegetable oil

2 large eggs

1 tbsp. whole kernel frozen corn, thawed

1 tsp. chopped roasted pepper in a jar

1 tsp. fresh salsa

2 tbsp. shredded pepper jack cheese

1/8 tsp. salt

1 slice 9-grain bread, toasted

Ground black pepper to taste

DIRECTIONS

Put vegetable oil in nonstick sauté pan. Take paper towel and wipe oil over surface of the pan, then wipe away excess. Place sauté pan over medium-high heat. Sauté corn and roasted peppers until fragrant, about 5 minutes.

Reduce heat to medium low. In a small bowl, whip eggs, salt and pepper with whisk or fork until blended. Add eggs to pan, stirring constantly with heat-resistant spatula. When eggs look set, slide on serving plate and top with fresh salsa and cheese. Serve with side of toast.

Prep time:	5 min.
Cook time:	10 min.
Total time:	15 min.
Yield:	1 serving
Serving size:	2 eggs, 4 tbsp. salsa mixture, 1 slice toast

TOTAL TIME 15 min.

TOTAL TIME 10 min.

Whole Wheat Breakfast Bruschetta with Scrambled Eggs, Goat Cheese, Sun-Dried Tomato & Fresh Basil

If you're a goat cheese enthusiast, our hearty and healthy Whole Wheat Breakfast Bruschetta with Scrambled Eggs, Goat Cheese, Sun-Dried Tomato & Fresh Basil is a no-brainer. Aside from the dish's antioxidant-rich sun-dried tomatoes, when it comes to fat and calories, goat cheese is a much healthier alternative to cheese made from cow's milk. Served with the toasted bruschetta, this is a dish that will have everyone scrambling for more!

INGREDIENTS

Cooking spray

8 large eggs

1/3 c. sliced sun-dried tomato

1/4 c. crumbled goat cheese

1 tbsp. chopped fresh basil

1/8 tsp. salt

8 slices whole wheat baguette, sliced on an angle and toasted

Ground black pepper to taste

DIRECTIONS

Spray a 10-inch nonstick skillet with cooking spray and place pan over medium heat.

In a medium-sized bowl, whisk eggs, salt and pepper together until blended. Add eggs to pan, stir the mixture with heat-resistant spatula until the eggs are softly set. Take pan off heat and fold in sun-dried tomato, goat cheese and basil. Divide eggs on four plates and serve with toasted baguette.

Prep time:	4 min.
Cook time:	5 min.
Total time:	10 min.
Yield:	4 servings
Serving size:	1/4 scrambled egg mixture, 2 slices baguette

NUTRITIONAL INFORMATION
Per Serving

Calories:	249
Total Fat:	13 g
Cholesterol:	377 mg
Sodium:	445 mg
Total Carbohydrates:	13 g
Fiber:	1 g
Sugars:	3 g
Protein:	16 g

Breakfast Veggie Burrito

Eating a burrito and counting calories — rarely the two ever meet. While a popular dish, burritos are often loaded with hidden fats and unhealthy ingredients. Our version of the breakfast burrito turns this less-than-desired option into a healthy meal without compromising on taste. Packed with fresh veggies, cheese and the must-have tortilla, it's an improvement on the original if we don't say so ourselves!

INGREDIENTS

Cooking spray
1/2 c. diced red bell pepper
8 large eggs
1/8 tsp. salt
1/3 c. shredded cheddar cheese
4 10" spinach tortillas
Ground black pepper to taste

DIRECTIONS

Spray a 10-inch nonstick skillet with cooking spray and heat pan over medium heat. Add bell pepper and sauté until softened, about 5 minutes.

Meanwhile, in a medium-sized bowl, whisk eggs, salt and pepper together until blended. Add eggs to pan, stir the mixture with heat-resistant spatula until the eggs are softly set. Take pan off heat and fold in cheddar cheese. Lay out tortillas and divide egg mixture between them. To assemble the burrito, fold bottom of tortilla over most of the filling, fold over sides and roll up. Repeat with remaining tortillas.

Prep time:	15 min.
Cook time:	5 min.
Total time:	20 min.
Yield:	4 servings
Serving size:	1 burrito

TOTAL TIME 20 min.

TOTAL TIME 10 min.

Egg White Omelet with Cucumber, Dill, Smoked Salmon & Whole Wheat Toast

This tasty omelet packs plenty of flavors with the chopped fresh dill and sliced cucumbers enhancing the salty smoked salmon.

We prefer English cucumbers – those long, skinny cukes you'll find wrapped in plastic at the supermarket, because they contain fewer seeds. If you can't find English cucumbers in your market, substitute regular cucumbers and remove the seeds.

INGREDIENTS

2 large egg whites

1/8 tsp. chopped fresh dill

1 tsp. vegetable oil

2 thin slices smoked salmon

2 1/8" wide slices unpeeled English cucumber

1 slice whole wheat bread, toasted

Salt and ground black pepper

DIRECTIONS

In small bowl, beat egg whites, dill, salt and pepper together with whisk or fork until well combined.

Place vegetable oil in nonstick sauté pan. With paper towel, spread oil over surface of pan, then wipe away excess. Place sauté pan over medium-low heat. Add egg mixture and cook for about 1 minute. Then flip omelet on reverse side to cook for about 10 seconds, using a spatula to help. Quickly place smoked salmon and cucumber on one half of omelet, folding other half atop them. Slide omelet out of pan onto plate. Serve with toast.

Prep time:	5 min.
Cook time:	5 min.
Total time:	10 min.
Yield:	1 serving
Serving size:	1 omelet
	1 slice toast

NUTRITIONAL INFORMATION
Per Serving

Calories:	307
Total Fat:	13 g
Cholesterol:	33 mg
Sodium:	634 mg
Total Carbohydrates:	26 g
Fiber:	4 g
Sugars:	6 g
Protein:	24 g

Asparagus Tarragon Omelet with Gruyére Cheese & Roasted Cherry Tomatoes

NUTRITIONAL INFORMATION
Per Serving

Calories:	234
Total Fat:	15 g
Cholesterol:	390 mg
Sodium:	497 mg
Total Carbohydrates:	5 g
Fiber:	2 g
Sugars:	2 g
Protein:	19 g

The delicate flavor of fresh tarragon is what makes this omelet sing; avoid using dried tarragon, which has no flavor. Roast the tomatoes and steam the asparagus the night before to make this breakfast even easier to pull together.

INGREDIENTS

3 asparagus spears
3 cherry tomatoes
2 large eggs
1/8 c. shredded Gruyére cheese
1/8 tbsp. chopped fresh tarragon
1/8 tsp. salt
1 tsp. vegetable oil
Ground black pepper to taste

DIRECTIONS

Place asparagus spears in a small microwaveable dish with 2 tablespoons of water and cover tightly with plastic. Microwave on high for 2 minutes. Allow the asparagus to sit for 2 minutes before removing the plastic. Set asparagus aside.

Adjust oven rack to upper-middle position and heat oven to 400 degrees. Line rimmed baking sheet with foil, place tomatoes on sheet and roast for 10 minutes, or until soft and beginning to fall apart. While tomatoes roast, chop asparagus into 1-inch pieces, combine with shredded Gruyére and tarragon, then set aside.

In small bowl, whisk eggs, salt and pepper together until thoroughly combined.

Place vegetable oil in small nonstick sauté pan. Take paper towel and wipe oil over surface of pan, wiping off any excess. Heat pan over medium-low heat, then add egg mixture. Let eggs cook for about 1 minute. With spatula, flip omelet on other side to cook for about 10 seconds. Put asparagus cheese, and tarragon mixture on half of omelet, folding other half over it. Slide omelet out of pan onto plate. Serve with roasted tomatoes.

Prep time:	5 min.
Cook time:	15 min.
Total time:	20 min.
Yield:	1 serving
Serving size:	1 omelet, 3 cherry tomatoes

TOTAL TIME 20 min.

TOTAL TIME 10 min.

Goat Cheese, Baby Spinach & Sun-Dried Tomato Omelet with Multi-Grain Toast

A classic breakfast with a Fresh Diet twist. Most people won't turn down a good omelet with toast for breakfast. But this particular breakfast gets a lot of special requests. Included in this recipe are some serious health heavyweights, like the spinach and multi grain toast, but the lesser-known champion is the sun-dried tomato. It brings a distinct flavor to this dish and is also a great source of vitamin C and iron. Now that's a power breakfast!

INGREDIENTS

1/3 c. baby spinach, chopped

2 tbsp. chopped sun-dried tomatoes

1 tbsp. crumbled goat cheese

2 large eggs

1 slice multi-grain bread, toasted

Ground black pepper, to taste

Cooking spray

DIRECTIONS

Combine baby spinach, sun-dried tomatoes and goat cheese in a small bowl and set aside.

In a separate small bowl, whisk eggs and pepper together until thoroughly combined.

Spray a small nonstick sauté pan with cooking spray. Heat pan over medium-low heat, then add egg mixture. Let eggs cook for about 1 minute, then flip omelet with a spatula. Cook for an additional 10 seconds. Put spinach and cheese mixture on one half of omelet and fold other half over filling. Slide omelet out of pan onto plate and serve with toasted multi-grain bread.

Prep time:	5 min.
Cook time:	5 min.
Total time:	10 min.
Yield:	1 serving
Serving size:	1 omelet,
	1 slice toast

NUTRITIONAL INFORMATION
Per Serving

Calories:	292
Total Fat:	14 g
Cholesterol:	377 mg
Sodium:	570 mg
Total Carbohydrates:	20 g
Fiber:	3 g
Sugars:	7 g
Protein:	18 g

Apricot Cream Cheese Crêpes
with Fresh Oranges & Raspberries

NUTRITIONAL INFORMATION
Per Serving

Calories:	458
Total Fat:	22 g
Cholesterol:	227 mg
Sodium:	586 mg
Total Carbohydrates:	50 g
Fiber:	4 g
Sugars:	24 g
Protein:	16 g

Thin, delicate crêpes can be difficult to make from scratch, which is why we love the premade ones you can find in your grocer's produce section.

INGREDIENTS

3 tbsp. reduced fat cream cheese

1/4 tsp. evaporated cane juice sugar

1 apricot, pitted and chopped into 1/4" pieces

2 crêpe shells

1 tsp. maple syrup

1/2 fresh orange, peeled and sectioned

4 fresh raspberries

DIRECTIONS

In small bowl, stir cream cheese, evaporated cane juice sugar and chopped apricots together until well combined.

Roll out crêpe shells and divide cream cheese filling between both, using a spoon to spread the filling over the crêpe. Fold two sides of crêpe toward center, and roll into a tube from one unfolded side. Top each crêpe with syrup and serve with orange and raspberries.

Prep time:	10 min.
Cook time:	0 min.
Total time:	10 min.
Yield:	1 serving
Serving size:	2 filled crêpes, 1/2 an orange, 4 raspberries

TOTAL TIME 10 min.

Ricotta Cheese Crêpes with Caramelized Bananas & Chocolate Sauce

We've always been proud that we can cook healthy food in a way that has most of our clients forgetting they are on a diet all together. But this particular breakfast, with its decadent ingredients and fabulous taste, really had beaming with pride. We believe eating well does not mean depriving oneself, and this breakfast is a testament to that.

NUTRITIONAL INFORMATION
Per Serving

Calories:	314
Total Fat:	11 g
Cholesterol:	66 mg
Sodium:	244 mg
Total Carbohydrates:	45 g
Fiber:	1 g
Sugars:	21 g
Protein:	8 g

INGREDIENTS

8 crêpe shells

1/2 c. part-skim ricotta cheese

1/2 tbsp. Smart Balance Buttery Spread

3 tbsp. light brown sugar

2 medium-small sized bananas, peeled and sliced

1 tbsp. chocolate syrup

banana slices gently, and cook for another minute. Divide bananas and sauce among four plates. Serve with prepared crêpes drizzled with chocolate syrup.

Prep time:	8 min.
Cook time:	2 min.
Total time:	10 min.
Yield:	4 servings
Serving size:	2 crêpes

DIRECTIONS

Lay crêpe shells out and divide ricotta cheese between them, using a spoon to spread the filling over the crêpes. Fold two sides of crêpe toward center, and roll up into a tube. Roll up remaining crêpes, and set aside.

Melt buttery spread in an 8-inch skillet over medium-high heat. Add brown sugar and lay banana slices on top. Cook for 1 minute, stir

Strawberry Stuffed Whole Wheat French Toast with Honeydew & Cinnamon Apple Yogurt

NUTRITIONAL INFORMATION
Per Serving

Calories:	303
Total Fat:	11 g
Cholesterol:	190 mg
Sodium:	286 mg
Total Carbohydrates:	40 g
Fiber:	4 g
Sugars:	16 g
Protein:	14 g

Cinnamon Apple Yogurt
NUTRITIONAL INFORMATION
Per Serving

Calories:	70
Total Fat:	1 g
Cholesterol:	3 mg
Sodium:	43 mg
Total Carbohydrates:	6 g
Fiber:	0 g
Sugars:	6 g
Protein:	3 g

Want to impress guests at breakfast? Stuffed French toast will do it every time, even though it's so easy to prepare! That's why we've included this recipe for a single serving. Treat yourself one morning, or double the recipe for two.

INGREDIENTS

1 large egg

1/2 tsp. vegetable oil

1/2 slice 1 1/2" thick whole wheat bread

1 fresh strawberry, sliced

1 tsp. maple syrup

1/4 c. fresh honeydew melon cut into 1/2" cubes

DIRECTIONS

In small bowl, whip egg with whisk or fork until blended.

Put vegetable oil in nonstick sauté pan. With paper towel, spread oil over surface of pan, then wipe away excess. Place sauté pan over medium-high heat. Dip bread in egg mixture while pan heats, allowing egg to soak into bread for about 1 minute. Place soaked bread in hot pan and cook for about 1 minute on both sides, until bread looks slightly crisp and golden brown. Remove bread to a serving plate.

Using small, sharp knife, cut a pocket horizontally into slice of bread. Stuff pocket with sliced strawberries. Serve with syrup on top, and melon and yogurt alongside.

INGREDIENTS Cinnamon Apple Yogurt

1/4 c. reduced fat plain yogurt

1 tbsp. chopped fresh apple

1/4 tsp. evaporated cane juice sugar

1/8 tsp. ground cinnamon

DIRECTIONS

In a small bowl combine yogurt, apple, sugar and cinnamon, and set aside.

Prep time:	15 min.
Cook time:	5 min.
Total time:	20 min.
Yield:	1 serving
Serving size:	1/2 stuffed French toast, 1/4 c. yogurt, 1/4 c. honeydew

TOTAL TIME 20 min.

TOTAL TIME 43 min.

Sweet Potato & Saffron Egg Frittata
with Chopped Scallions & Italian Parsley

Saffron is the world's most expensive spice, but luckily, it works best when used with a frugal hand. A small amount imparts its distinctive, earthy flavor and yellow hue into this frittata.

Sweet potatoes are packed with nutrients like vitamins A and C and help stabilize blood sugar, which makes them the perfect food to begin the day.

INGREDIENTS

6 large eggs

3/4 c. finely chopped scallions

1 tbsp. finely chopped
   Italian parsley

1/2 tsp. saffron

1/2 tsp. salt

1/4 tsp. ground black pepper

2 6 to 8 oz. sweet potatoes,
   peeled and sliced 1/8" thick

DIRECTIONS

Adjust oven rack to upper-middle position and heat oven to 350 degrees. Spray 9-inch round ovenproof dish with cooking spray.

In large bowl, mix eggs, scallions, parsley, saffron, salt and ground pepper together; set bowl aside for 15 minutes to let flavors mingle.

Meanwhile, lay sweet potato slices evenly around bottom of ovenproof dish, spray with cooking oil, and bake for 10 minutes. Remove dish from oven.

Give egg mixture quick stir to awaken saffron flavor, then pour over sweet potatoes. Return ovenproof dish to oven and bake for 20-25 minutes total, spraying surface of frittata with cooking spray midway through baking to create a crisp surface. (Frittata will continue to cook and firm up once removed from the oven.) Allow frittata to cool for 10 minutes before cutting into six slices.

Prep time:	8 min.
Cook time:	35 min.
Total time:	43 min.
Yield:	6 servings
Serving size:	1 wedge

NUTRITIONAL INFORMATION
Per Serving

Calories:	458
Total Fat:	22 g
Cholesterol:	227 mg
Sodium:	586 mg
Total Carbohydrates:	50 g
Fiber:	4 g
Sugars:	24 g
Protein:	16 g

Oregano, Zucchini & Mozzarella Cheese Quiche with Fresh Pineapple

NUTRITIONAL INFORMATION
Per Serving

Calories:	142
Total Fat:	7 g
Cholesterol:	192 mg
Sodium:	376 mg
Total Carbohydrates:	9 g
Fiber:	2 g
Sugars:	7 g
Protein:	10 g

Some think bacon and eggs are the perfect marriage, but we think zucchini and eggs make real culinary magic, especially with the flavor boost of Parmesan cheese.

INGREDIENTS

1/2 tsp. vegetable oil

6 c. chopped zucchini cut into 1/2" pieces

1/2 tsp. salt

1/4 tsp. ground black pepper

6 large eggs

1/2 c. shredded fresh Parmesan cheese

1 1/2 c. chopped fresh pineapple cut into 1/2" pieces

Cooking spray

DIRECTIONS

Adjust oven rack to upper-middle position and heat oven to 350 degrees.

Place vegetable oil in a nonstick sauté pan. With paper towel, spread oil over surface of the pan and wipe off excess. Heat sauté pan over medium-high heat and add zucchini once pan is hot. Stir occasionally and cook until light golden brown, approximately 10 minutes. Remove from heat, sprinkle with salt and pepper, and set aside to cool for another 10 minutes.

Spray 9-inch ovenproof round pan with cooking spray, and arrange cooled zucchini around bottom. In a small bowl, whisk eggs together with whisk or fork. Pour eggs over zucchini and top with Parmesan cheese. Bake for 30-40 minutes, or until center of egg bake is just firm. Let cool for 5-10 minutes before cutting into six slices. Serve with pineapple.

Prep time:	8 min.
Cook time:	50 min.
Total time:	58 min.
Yield:	6 servings
Serving size:	1 wedge, 1/4 c. pineapple

TOTAL TIME 58 min.

TOTAL TIME 48 min.

Portobello Mushroom, Shallot & Parmesan Cheese Egg Bake with Fresh Papaya

Here's a breakfast dish that feels both filling – thanks to the eggs and cheese – and light, thanks to the fresh papaya. Papaya, like pineapple, contains bromelain, which helps digest proteins, making it an ideal complement to egg recipes.

INGREDIENTS

6 large eggs

3 c. chopped portobello mushrooms

1/2 c. chopped shallots

3/4 c. shredded fresh Parmesan cheese

1/2 tsp. salt

1/4 tsp. ground black pepper

1 1/2 c. diced fresh papaya

Cooking spray

DIRECTIONS

Adjust oven rack to upper-middle position and heat oven to 325 degrees. Spray 9-inch round ovenproof dish with cooking spray.

In a small bowl, whisk eggs until blended. Put mushrooms in dish, then top with chopped shallots. Season with salt and pepper and bake for 10 minutes. Remove dish from oven, top vegetable mixture with cheese and slowly pour eggs over all. Return dish to oven and bake for another 25-30 minutes, or until center of egg bake is just firm. It will continue to cook after pan is removed from the oven.

Let egg bake cool for 10 minutes before cutting into six equal portions. Serve with diced papaya.

Prep time:	8 min.
Cook time:	40 min.
Total time:	48 min.
Yield:	6 servings
Serving size:	1 wedge, 1/4 c. papaya

NUTRITIONAL INFORMATION
Per Serving

Calories:	139
Total Fat:	8 g
Cholesterol:	193 mg
Sodium:	441 mg
Total Carbohydrates:	6 g
Fiber:	1 g
Sugars:	4 g
Protein:	11 g

Swiss Chard, Oyster Mushroom & Mozzarella Egg Bake with Fresh Pear

Starting your day with eggs is always a good idea. Not only are eggs a great source of protein, they also make you feel full and satisfied longer. Putting the obvious health benefits aside, the tasty combination of fresh fruit and vegetables paired with cheesy goodness make this breakfast a real crowd pleaser.

NUTRITIONAL INFORMATION
Per Serving

Calories:	160
Total Fat:	9 g
Cholesterol:	193 m
Sodium:	361 mg
Total Carbohydrates:	9 g
Fiber:	2 g
Sugars:	4 g
Protein:	11 g

INGREDIENTS

6 large eggs

2 c. chopped Swiss chard, stems and center ribs removed

1 c. chopped oyster mushrooms

3/4 c. shredded part-skim mozzarella

1/2 tsp. salt

1/4 tsp. ground black pepper

1 1/2 c. sliced fresh pear

Cooking spray

DIRECTIONS

Adjust oven rack to upper-middle position and heat oven to 325 degrees. Spray 9-inch round ovenproof dish with cooking spray.

In a small bowl, whisk eggs until blended and set aside. Place Swiss chard and mushrooms in prepared dish, season with salt and pepper, and bake for 10 minutes. Remove dish from oven, sprinkle vegetable mixture with cheese, and slowly pour eggs on top. Return dish to oven and bake for another 25-30 minutes, or until center of egg bake is just firm. It will continue to cook after pan is removed from the oven.

Let egg bake cool for 10 minutes before cutting into six equal portions. Serve with pear slices.

Prep time:	8 min.
Cook time:	40 min.
Total time:	48 min.
Yield:	6 servings
Serving size:	1 wedge, 1/4 c. pear

TOTAL TIME 48 min.

LUNCH

LIGHT YET FILLING RECIPES TO POWER YOU
THROUGH THE AFTERNOON

Fresh Bocconcini Mozzarella Salad with Roasted Yellow Bell Pepper, Tomato, Black Bean, Romaine Lettuce & Red Wine Vinaigrette

NUTRITIONAL INFORMATION
Per Serving

Calories:	319
Total Fat:	21 g
Cholesterol:	10 mg
Sodium:	356 mg
Total Carbohydrates:	27 g
Fiber:	3 g
Sugars:	7 g
Protein:	10 g

Red Wine Vinaigrette
NUTRITIONAL INFORMATION
Per Serving

Calories:	145
Total Fat:	16 g
Cholesterol:	12 mg
Sodium:	275 mg
Total Carbohydrates:	0 g
Fiber:	0 g
Sugars:	0 g
Protein:	0 g

Bocconcini means "little mouthful" because they are soft "little mouthfuls of mozzarella." We like to call them "little mouthfuls of heaven" because when they're combined with the bell peppers, black beans and our tart red wine vinaigrette, that's exactly what they are!

Store the Bocconcini in the fridge in its own liquid. It will keep for up to three weeks if you replace the water every couple of days with cooled boiled water and a pinch of sea salt.

INGREDIENTS

8 c. chopped romaine lettuce

12 oz. fresh Bocconcini mozzarella (grape sized)

1 yellow bell pepper, sliced into match-stick size strips

8 cherry tomatoes

1 c. canned black beans, drained and rinsed

2/3 c. Red Wine Vinaigrette (recipe follows)

DIRECTIONS

Place all ingredients in a large mixing bowl and toss to coat evenly. Divide salad among four bowls and serve.

Prep time:	10 min.
Cook time:	0 min.
Total time:	10 min.
Yield:	4 servings
Serving size:	1/4 of salad

INGREDIENTS Red Wine Vinaigrette

1/4 c. red wine vinegar

1 tsp. kosher salt

1/4 tsp. fresh ground black pepper

2 tsp. Dijon mustard

2/3 c. extra virgin olive oil

1 tbsp. minced fresh Italian parsley

1 tbsp. minced fresh basil

DIRECTIONS

Combine vinegar, salt, black pepper and mustard in blender jar. Blend on medium speed while pouring oil slowly through lid opening; blend until dressing is smooth and creamy. Pour dressing into a small bowl and stir in the minced herbs. Mix before serving.

Prep time:	5 min.
Cook time:	0 min.
Total time:	5 min.
Yield:	6 servings
Serving size:	3 tbsp.

TOTAL TIME 10 min.

TOTAL TIME 25 min.

Baby Spinach Salad with Marinated Shiitake Mushrooms, Red Onion, Radicchio, Grilled Chicken & Port Wine Vinaigrette

There is no reason that your daily lunch shouldn't contain just as much character as its more spoiled mealtime counterpart – dinner. While it is often the case because less time is devoted to preparing lunches, our Marinated Shiitake Mushroom and Spinach Salad recipe provides a simple yet satisfying solution to this conundrum. It doesn't take long to make but it does pack some powerful flavor!

If you'd rather not use wine in the vinaigrette, you can substitute with red wine vinegar.

INGREDIENTS

1 c. sliced shiitake mushrooms

2/3 c. Port Wine Vinaigrette (recipe follows)

4 c. diced, grilled chicken breast

3 c. baby spinach

4 c. shredded radicchio

1/2 c. diced red onion

DIRECTIONS

In small mixing bowl, combine mushrooms with vinaigrette and set aside to marinate for 15-20 minutes.

While mushrooms are marinating, place the remaining ingredients in a large bowl. Add mushrooms along with vinaigrette to bowl and toss to coat evenly. Divide salad among four bowls and serve.

Prep time:	25 min.
Cook time:	0 min.
Total time:	25 min.
Yield:	4 servings
Serving size:	1/4 of salad

INGREDIENTS Port Wine Vinaigrette

2 1/2 tbsp. port wine

1/4 c. red wine vinegar

1/2 tsp. salt

1/4 tsp. ground black pepper

2 tbsp. light brown sugar

2/3 c. salad oil
   (75% vegetable oil, 25% olive oil)

DIRECTIONS

Combine port, vinegar, salt and black pepper in blender jar. Blend on medium speed while pouring oil slowly through lid opening; blend until dressing is smooth and creamy. Mix before serving to blend oil into the dressing.

Prep time:	5 min.
Cook time:	0 min.
Total time:	5 min.
Yield:	6 servings
Serving size:	3 tbsp.

NUTRITIONAL INFORMATION
Per Serving

Calories:	394
Total Fat:	18 g
Cholesterol:	119 mg
Sodium:	247 mg
Total Carbohydrates:	9 g
Fiber:	2 g
Sugars:	3 g
Protein:	45 g

Port Wine Vinaigrette
NUTRITIONAL INFORMATION
Per Serving

Calories:	164
Total Fat:	16 g
Cholesterol:	0 mg
Sodium:	125 mg
Total Carbohydrates:	4 g
Fiber:	0 g
Sugars:	3 g
Protein:	0 g

Chicken Salad with Baby Spinach, Blackberries, Orange Segments, Pistachio & Mango Poppy Dressing

Here's a fun variation on the standard chicken salad. Rather than making it with greens and the classic salad vegetables — tomato, onions, carrots, celery —use fresh fruit like blackberries, orange and mango to edge this salad into another dimension. You'll get a generous four servings out of the dressing; the remaining dressing can be refrigerated for up to five days.

Look for canned or frozen mango pulp in your grocer's international foods aisle or frozen food section.

NUTRITIONAL INFORMATION
Per Serving

Calories:	420
Total Fat:	16 g
Cholesterol:	96 mg
Sodium:	389 mg
Total Carbohydrates:	26 g
Fiber:	9 g
Sugars:	13 g
Protein:	43 g

Mango Poppy Seed Dressing
NUTRITIONAL INFORMATION
Per Serving

Calories:	180
Total Fat:	15 g
Cholesterol:	0 mg
Sodium:	240 mg
Total Carbohydrates:	12 g
Fiber:	1 g
Sugars:	11 g
Protein:	0 g

INGREDIENTS

8 c. chopped romaine lettuce

12 oz. fresh Bocconcini mozzarella (grape sized)

1 yellow bell pepper, sliced into match-stick size strips

8 cherry tomatoes

1 c. canned black beans, drained and rinsed

2/3 c. Red Wine Vinaigrette (recipe follows)

DIRECTIONS

In small mixing bowl, combine all ingredients except blackberries and mix gently to coat with dressing evenly. Place salad on serving plate and top with blackberries.

Prep time:	10 min.
Cook time:	0 min.
Total time:	10 min.
Yield:	1 serving
Serving size:	1 salad

INGREDIENTS Mango Poppy Seed Dress

1/2 c. mango pulp

3 tbsp. light brown sugar, lightly pack

1/2 tsp. salt

1/4 tsp. mustard

1/4 tsp. onion powder

1/4 tsp. garlic powder

1/4 c. cider vinegar

1/2 tbsp. lemon juice

1/3 c. salad oil (75% vegetable oil /25% olive oil)

2 tsp. poppy seeds

DIRECTIONS

Combine mango pulp, sugar, salt, mustard, onion powder, garlic powder, cider vinegar and lemon juice in blender jar. Mix on medium speed while pouring oil slowly through lid opening; blend until dressing is smooth and creamy. Pour dressing into small bowl and stir in poppy seeds. Mix before serving to blend oil into dressing.

Prep time:	5 min.
Cook time:	0 min.
Total time:	5 min.
Yield:	6 servings
Serving size:	3 tbsp.

TOTAL TIME **10** min.

TOTAL TIME 7 min.

Maple Glazed Ham Salad with Diced Pears, Toasted Walnuts, Dried Cherries, Baby Lettuce & Raspberry Vinaigrette

I think of this salad as a winter salad, but it's delicious year-round and makes good use of any leftover ham in your fridge. If you can't find dried cherries, dried cranberries make a delicious substitute.

INGREDIENTS

1/2 tbsp. seedless raspberry jam

1 tbsp. white wine vinegar

1 tsp. Dijon mustard

1 1/2 tbsp. extra virgin olive oil

1/8 tsp. black pepper

2 c. baby lettuce

1/2 c. maple-glazed ham, chopped into 1/4" cubes (4 oz.)

1/4 c. diced fresh pear, chopped into 1/4" cubes

2 tbsp. toasted walnut pieces*

2 tbsp. dried cherries

DIRECTIONS

Whisk jam, vinegar, mustard, olive oil and pepper in a medium sized bowl until smooth. Add remaining ingredients to the bowl, and mix gently so the vinaigrette coats evenly. Place salad on plate and serve.

*Toast walnuts by placing into small skillet set over medium heat. Cook until nuts are deeper brown and fragrant, about 4 to 5 minutes. Stir them around pan frequently to toast on all sides. Remove nuts from pan to cool completely before serving.

Prep time:	7 min.
Cook time:	0 min.
Total time:	7 min.
Yield:	1 serving
Serving size:	1 salad

NUTRITIONAL INFORMATION
Per Serving

Calories:	537
Total Fat:	33 g
Cholesterol:	40 mg
Sodium:	1168 mg
Total Carbohydrates:	41 g
Fiber:	4 g
Sugars:	21 g
Protein:	24 g

Crispy Baked Goat Cheese Medallions with Mesclun Lettuce, Sliced Pears, Toasted Almonds & Raspberry Dressing

NUTRITIONAL INFORMATION
Per Serving

Calories:	376
Total Fat:	27 g
Cholesterol:	15 mg
Sodium:	454 mg
Total Carbohydrates:	31 g
Fiber:	6 g
Sugars:	15 g
Protein:	5 g

Mesclun is simply a mix of young salad greens, including arugula, sorrel, dandelion, mizuma, mache, radicchio and other tender leaves. Choose crisp-looking mesclun with no signs of wilt, and store in a plastic bag in the produce bin of your refrigerator.

Toast sliced almonds in a small skillet set over medium-high heat for 2 minutes to heighten flavor.

INGREDIENTS

1 3/4" wide slice of goat cheese
1 tbsp. corn flake crumbs
1/2 tbsp. seedless raspberry jam
1 tbsp. white wine vinegar
1 tsp. Dijon mustard
1 1/2 tbsp. extra virgin olive oil
1/8 tsp. salt
1/8 tsp. black pepper
2 c. mesclun
3 1/4" wide slices of fresh pear
1 tbsp. sliced almonds

DIRECTIONS

Adjust oven rack to upper-middle position and heat oven to 350 degrees.

Press corn flake crumbs around sides of goat cheese. Place in oven-proof dish and bake for 10-12 minutes until crumbs start to brown and cheese begins to soften. Remove cheese round from oven and chill in refrigerator until completely cooled, approximately 2 hours.

When ready to serve, whisk jam, vinegar, mustard, olive oil, salt and pepper in a medium-sized bowl until smooth. Add mesclun to the bowl, and mix gently so the vinaigrette coats evenly. Place dressed greens on a plate, and top with pear slices, almonds and chilled goat cheese medallion.

Prep time:	5 min.
Cook time:	12 min.
Total time:	17 min.
Yield:	1 serving
Serving size:	1 salad, 1 medallion

TOTAL TIME **17** min.

TOTAL TIME 40 min.

Hearty Lentil, Turkey Sausage, & Brown Rice Soup

On a cold, blustery autumn day, this is the comforting, stick-to-your-ribs kind of soup you'll savor. With just five ingredients, it's easy to make, and the smoky sausage gives it surprising depth of flavor.

INGREDIENTS

2 turkey breakfast sausage links

2 c. reduced-sodium chicken broth

1 c. water

2 tbsp. yellow lentils

1 tbsp. medium-grain brown rice

DIRECTIONS

Adjust oven rack to upper-middle position and heat oven to 350 degrees. Place oven-proof cooling rack onto foil-lined rimmed baking sheet. Place sausage on cooling rack and bake for 15 minutes until browned and sizzling. Remove from oven and cut into 1/2-inch pieces when cool enough to touch.

While sausages are cooking, combine chicken broth, water and lentils in medium saucepan set over medium-high heat. Bring to a boil, then reduce heat to bring liquid to a simmer and cook for 15 minutes. Add brown rice and cook for an additional 15-20 minutes until rice and lentils are tender. Add sausage slices to soup and serve.

Prep time:	0 min.
Cook time:	40 min.
Total time:	40 min.
Yield:	1 serving
Serving size:	1 1/2 c. soup

NUTRITIONAL INFORMATION
Per Serving

Calories:	291
Total Fat:	8 g
Cholesterol:	37 mg
Sodium:	509 mg
Total Carbohydrates:	29 g
Fiber:	8 g
Sugars:	1 g
Protein:	27 g

Cajun Shrimp Stuffed Portobello Mushroom Crowns with Balsamic Reduction Sauce

NUTRITIONAL INFORMATION
Per Serving

Calories:	136
Total Fat:	1 g
Cholesterol:	44 mg
Sodium:	244 mg
Total Carbohydrates:	26 g
Fiber:	1 g
Sugars:	24 g
Protein:	7 g

Balsamic Reduction

NUTRITIONAL INFORMATION
Per Serving

Calories:	92
Total Fat:	0 g
Cholesterol:	0 mg
Sodium:	8 mg
Total Carbohydrates:	23 g
Fiber:	0 g
Sugars:	22 g
Protein:	0 g

This recipe – a favorite with our clients – requires just a few ingredients and is simple to prepare. Make the balsamic reduction first, as you'll need it to cook the mushrooms. And speaking of mushrooms, look for portobello caps that feel firm and slightly damp; avoid those that are slimy to the touch or have soft spots.

INGREDIENTS

4 4" portobello mushrooms, wiped with a damp paper towel and stems removed

1 recipe Balsamic Reduction (recipe follows)

20 raw shrimp, 16/20 per pound, peeled with tails off

1/2 tsp. Cajun-style seasoning

DIRECTIONS

Adjust oven rack to upper-middle position and heat oven to 350 degrees. Line rimmed baking sheet with foil and place mushroom caps on foil with gills facing up. Drizzle each cap with 1 tablespoon Balsamic Reduction. Place 5 shrimp on each mushroom cap. Bake for 20 minutes. Drizzle remaining Balsamic Reduction across mushrooms before serving.

Prep time:	5 min.
Cook time:	20 min.
Total time:	25 min.
Yield:	4 servings
Serving size:	1 stuffed mushroom

INGREDIENTS Balsamic Reduction

1/2 c. balsamic vinegar

1/4 c. honey

1/4 tsp. corn starch

DIRECTIONS

In small saucepan set over medium-high heat, combine all ingredients and bring to boil. Reduce heat and simmer for 10 minutes until slightly thickened and reduced by half.

Prep time:	0 min.
Cook time:	10 min.
Total time:	10 min.
Yield:	4 servings
Serving size:	3/4 tbsp. reduction

TOTAL TIME 25 min.

TOTAL TIME 7 min.

Crab Salad Sandwich on Nine-Grain Bread
with Celery, Tomato & Lettuce

If you can get fresh crab in your market – wonderful! But pasteurized crab claw meat works nicely in this special lunchtime treat, and it's often available in your supermarket's refrigerated seafood section.

INGREDIENTS

2/3 c. fresh or pasteurized crab meat (8 oz.)

4 tbsp. fat-free mayonnaise

2 tbsp. reduced-fat sour cream

1 tbsp. chopped celery

1/4 tsp. salt

1/8 tsp. ground pepper

2 slices nine-grain bread

1/2 c. shredded romaine lettuce

2 slices of tomato, cut 1/4" thick

DIRECTIONS

In small mixing bowl, combine crab meat, mayonnaise, sour cream, celery, salt and pepper, and stir to combine thoroughly.

Place one slice of bread on a cutting board. Spread crab salad across bread, then top with lettuce and tomato before covering with remaining slice of bread. Cut sandwich in half and serve.

Prep time: 7 min.
Cook time: 0 min.
Total time: 7 min.
Yield: 2 servings
Serving size: 1/2 sandwich

NUTRITIONAL INFORMATION
Per Serving

Calories:	273
Total Fat:	6 g
Cholesterol:	56 mg
Sodium:	1734 mg
Total Carbohydrates:	29 g
Fiber:	3 g
Sugars:	5 g
Protein:	27 g

Roasted Eggplant & Havarti Cheese Sandwich on Whole Wheat Bread with Bell Pepper Pesto & Baby Lettuce

NUTRITIONAL INFORMATION
Per Serving

Calories:	324
Total Fat:	16 g
Cholesterol:	31 mg
Sodium:	786 mg
Total Carbohydrates:	29 g
Fiber:	6 g
Sugars:	4 g
Protein:	13 g

A lot of home cooks are afraid of cooking eggplant, which is a shame because it's one of the "meatier" fruits out there. In fact, it's actually a berry! Just use a light hand with the oil (eggplant absorbs oil like a sponge) and look for fruits that are firm, glossy and heavy for their size.

INGREDIENTS

6 1/4" wide slices of eggplant
Cooking spray
1/4 tsp. salt
1/8 tsp. ground black pepper
4 slices Havarti cheese
2 slices whole wheat bread
1/2 c. baby lettuce
1 serving Bell Pepper Pesto
  (recipe follows)

DIRECTIONS

Adjust oven rack to upper-middle position and heat oven to 400 degrees. Line rimmed baking sheet with foil.

Lay eggplant slices down on the foil and spray both sides lightly with cooking spray, then sprinkle with salt and pepper. Bake for 10-15 minutes until eggplant is golden brown and fragrant. Remove from oven to cool before handling. Spread bell pepper pesto across one slice of bread and top with baby lettuce.

Place two slices eggplant on the lettuce, and top with two slices of cheese; repeat with remaining eggplant and cheese. Place remaining slice of bread on top, cut sandwich in half, and serve.

Prep time:	6 min.
Cook time:	15 min.
Total time:	21 min.
Yield:	2 servings
Serving size:	1/2 sandwich

INGREDIENTS Bell Pepper Pesto

2 tbsp. chopped jarred roasted
  red bell peppers
4 fresh basil leaves, chopped finely
1 tsp. extra virgin olive oil
Pinch of salt and ground black pepper

DIRECTIONS

Add all ingredients to a small bowl and mix well to combine.

Prep time:	5 min.
Cook time:	0 min.
Total time:	5 min.
Yield:	2 servings
Serving size:	1 tbsp.

TOTAL TIME 21 min.

TOTAL TIME **18** min.

Seared Tofu Wrap with Alfalfa Sprouts, Snow Peas, Watercress, Baby Lettuce & Soy Dressing

You don't have to be a vegetarian to consider adding tofu to your diet. Our Asian-inspired tofu wrap is a bouquet of clean flavors that really showcases the exquisite potential of tofu and what it can add to a diet.

Tofu is extremely nutritious and has many health benefits. Just eating two grams of it daily can help your body reduce the cholesterol it absorbs by more than 10%. It's low in fat, calories and cholesterol and is also an excellent source of high-quality protein.

INGREDIENTS

1 (1 lb.) package extra firm tofu, drained, pressed, and diced

1/2 c. honey soy marinade (recipe follows)

1 c. snow peas, strings removed

1 c. chopped watercress leaves

1 1/2 c. alfalfa sprouts

4 whole wheat wraps, approx. 10" diameter

DIRECTIONS

Heat a 12-inch non stick skillet over medium-high heat. Add tofu and marinade and sauté for 10 minutes, until tofu is golden brown. Set aside and let cool before assembling wraps.

Divide tofu, snow peas, watercress and alfalfa sprouts between the wraps. Fold bottom of wrap over most of the filling, fold over sides, and roll up. Repeat with remaining wraps.

Serve with remaining soy honey marinade for dipping, if desired.

Prep time:	8 min.
Cook time:	10 min.
Total time:	18 min.
Yield:	4 servings
Serving size:	1 wrap

INGREDIENTS Soy Honey Marinade

1/3 c. less sodium soy sauce

1/3 c. salad oil blend (75% vegetable oil, 25% olive oil)

2 tbsp. rice vinegar

1/3 c. honey

DIRECTIONS

Combine all ingredients in a medium-sized bowl and whisk until blended.

Prep time:	5 min.
Cook time:	0 min.
Total time:	5 min.
Yield:	9 servings
Serving size:	2 tbsp.

NUTRITIONAL INFORMATION
Per Serving

Calories:	441
Total Fat:	19 g
Cholesterol:	0 mg
Sodium:	860 mg
Total Carbohydrates:	49 g
Fiber:	2 g
Sugars:	11 g
Protein:	19 g

Soy Honey Marinade
NUTRITIONAL INFORMATION
Per Serving

Calories:	116
Total Fat:	8 g
Cholesterol:	0 mg
Sodium:	345 mg
Total Carbohydrates:	11 g
Fiber:	0 g
Sugars:	10 g
Protein:	0 g

Mushroom Souffle & Gruyère Cheese Panini on Whole Wheat Ciabatta Bread

NUTRITIONAL INFORMATION
Per Serving

Calories:	294
Total Fat:	15 g
Cholesterol:	38 mg
Sodium:	457 mg
Total Carbohydrates:	21 g
Fiber:	2 g
Sugars:	2 g
Protein:	14 g

Like most people, we appreciate a good sandwich. But of course, if it's coming from our kitchens, we've added fine flair to give it our signature Fresh Diet sparkle. We've shaken up a classic panini recipe by adding a sophisticated cheese like Gruyère and an old classic, the mushroom duxelle. The result is a taste that is a little bit sweet, slightly salty and very delicious! If you prefer, you can substitute the wine in this recipe with chicken or veggie broth.

Please note that this recipe has been written without the inclusion of a panini press, however if you have one available, feel free to use it to simplify the preparation.

INGREDIENTS

- 1 tbsp. extra-virgin olive oil
- 8 oz. button mushrooms, stems removed and finely chopped
- 1 tbsp. fresh thyme
- 1/4 tsp. kosher salt
- 1/8 tsp. ground black pepper
- 1/3 c. dry white wine
- 1 c. shredded Gruyère cheese
- 4 4"x4" whole wheat ciabatta rolls
- Cooking spray

DIRECTIONS

Heat oil in a 10" non-stick skillet over medium heat; add the mushrooms and thyme and sauté for 10 minutes while stirring often. Season mixture with salt and pepper and stir in white wine; cook for an additional 10 minutes until all liquid has been reduced. Transfer to a bowl and let cool before stirring in gruyere.

Heat a large grill pan over medium-high heat. Split ciabatta rolls in half horizontally; divide duxelle mixture evenly between bottoms and cover with roll tops.

Spray griddle with cooking spray and place sandwiches in pan (this might have to be done in batches depending on size of grill pan). Spray tops with cooking spray and press sandwiches down with a heavy skillet. Cook for 4 minutes per side. Transfer sandwiches to a cutting board and let cool 5 minutes before slicing in half.

Prep time:	6 min.
Cook time:	28 min.
Total time:	34 min.
Yield:	4 servings
Serving size:	1 sandwich

TOTAL TIME **34** min.

TOTAL TIME 18 min.

Philly Cheese Steak Whole Wheat Wrap
with Sautéed Bell Pepper & Mozzarella Cheese

We are renowned for many of our dishes, but none so popular as our famed Philly Cheese Steak Wrap. Most people assume that the arrival of a diet means a fond farewell to calorie-dense dishes like the cheese steak. But by preparing this lunch the way Chef Yos instructs, there is no need to say goodbye to a meal this good!

You'll notice that this recipe mentions putting the steak in the freezer before working with it. Because if the meat is firm, it is a lot easier to slice. About 30-40 minutes in the freezer is sufficient.

INGREDIENTS

1/2 lb. strip loin

1 tbsp. extra-virgin olive oil

1 red bell pepper, sliced

1/4 tsp. kosher salt, divided

1/4 tsp. ground black pepper, divided

4 whole wheat tortillas, approx. 10" diameter

1 c. shredded part-skim mozzarella cheese

DIRECTIONS

Place the steak in the freezer. Heat oil in a 10-inch non stick skillet over medium-high heat. Add peppers, 1/8 teaspoon salt and 1/8 teaspoon black pepper and sauté until the peppers are soft. Transfer peppers to a plate and set aside. Remove the meat from the freezer and slice thinly across the grain. In the same skillet over medium-high heat add the sliced steak, season with remaining salt and pepper and sauté for 1-2 minutes. To assemble a wrap, lay tortillas out. Place a quarter of the beef mixture and sautéed peppers on the bottom edge of each tortilla and top each with a 1/4 cup of cheese. Fold bottom of tortilla over most of the filling, fold over sides and roll up. Repeat with remaining tortillas.

Prep time:	8 min
Cook time:	10 min
Total time:	18 min
Yield:	4 servings
Serves:	1 wrap

NUTRITIONAL INFORMATION
Per Serving

Calories:	406
Total Fat:	16 g
Cholesterol:	44 mg
Sodium:	842 mg
Total Carbohydrates:	36 g
Fiber:	0 g
Sugars:	1 g
Protein:	27 g

Tarragon-Infused Salmon & Cheddar Cheese Melt on Whole Wheat Wrap

NUTRITIONAL INFORMATION
Per Serving

Calories:	375
Total Fat:	18 g
Cholesterol:	92 mg
Sodium:	836 mg
Total Carbohydrates:	24 g
Fiber:	8 g
Sugars:	3 g
Protein:	35 g

Tarragon is usually paired with chicken, but we think its delicate anise-like flavor works wonderfully with a stronger-flavored fish, like salmon. Always use fresh tarragon in your cooking; dried tarragon offers no flavor.

Salmon is a terrific source of omega-3 fatty acids, which promote heart health.

INGREDIENTS

8 oz. salmon filet

1/2 c. shredded cheddar cheese

2 whole wheat tortillas,
   approx. 10" diameter

1/2 tsp. chopped fresh tarragon

1/4 tsp. salt

1/8 tsp. ground black pepper

DIRECTIONS

Adjust an oven rack to upper-middle position and heat oven to 350 degrees.

Place salmon filet skin-side down on foil-lined baking sheet. Rub tarragon over fish, then season with salt and pepper. Bake for 8-10 minutes until fish is just cooked through, then remove from oven and let cool.

When salmon is cool enough to touch, use your fingers to flake and crumble it into a medium mixing bowl. Add shredded cheddar and use your hands to gently mix ingredients together.

To assemble a wrap, lay tortillas out. Place 1/2 the salmon mixture on the bottom edge of each tortilla. Fold bottom of tortilla over most of the filling, fold over sides and roll up. Repeat with remaining tortilla.

Prep time:	8 min.
Cook time:	10 min.
Total time:	18 min.
Yield:	2 servings
Serving size:	1/2 wrap

TOTAL TIME **18** min.

TOTAL TIME **16** min.

Grilled Lamb Burger on Whole Wheat Bun
with Yellow Tomato & Mint Aioli

If you're iffy about lamb, get a little adventurous and try a ground lamb burger – you'll find its flavor and juiciness a delicious option to beef. Yellow tomatoes are a nice change from the standard red ones, and tend to be lower in acid, too. Mint is a classic pairing with lamb – this burger simply sings with the aioli !

INGREDIENTS

1 lb. ground lamb

1 large egg

1 tbsp. corn flake crumbs

1/4 tsp. salt

1/8 tsp. ground black pepper

4 whole wheat hamburger buns

1 c. shredded romaine lettuce

4 1/4" slices yellow tomato

DIRECTIONS

Preheat gas or charcoal grill according to manufacturer's directions, or heat small grill pan over medium heat.

In a small bowl, combine ground lamb, egg, corn flake crumbs, salt and pepper. Divide evenly into fourths and shape four burgers. Grill burgers for approximately 4-5 minutes on each side, or until slightly pink in center.

Spread aioli on bottom half of each bun. Assemble burgers by placing romaine on bottom bun, topped by burger, a slice of tomato, and remaining half of bun.

Prep time:	6 min.
Cook time:	10 min.
Total time:	16 min.
Yield:	4 servings
Serving size:	1 burger

INGREDIENTS Mint Aioli

8 tbsp. fat-free mayonnaise

1 tsp. minced garlic

1 tsp. extra virgin olive oil

1/2 tsp. chopped fresh mint

Salt and ground black pepper to taste

DIRECTIONS

Combine mayonnaise, garlic, olive oil and mint in small bowl and mix well. Add salt and pepper to taste.

Prep time:	5 min.
Cook time:	0 min.
Total time:	5 min.
Yield:	4 servings
Serving size:	2 tbsp.

NUTRITIONAL INFORMATION
Per Serving

Calories:	522
Total Fat:	31 g
Cholesterol:	130 mg
Sodium:	746 mg
Total Carbohydrates:	36 g
Fiber:	8 g
Sugars:	4 g
Protein:	28 g

Mint Aioli
NUTRITIONAL INFORMATION
Per Serving

Calories:	9
Total Fat:	1 g
Cholesterol:	1 mg
Sodium:	133 mg
Total Carbohydrates:	1 g
Fiber:	0 g
Sugars:	1 g
Protein:	0 g

Thai Turkey Burger on Whole Wheat Ciabatta with Sautéed Bok-Choy & Peanut Sauce

NUTRITIONAL INFORMATION
Per Serving

Calories:	287
Total Fat:	4 g
Cholesterol:	65 mg
Sodium:	957 mg
Total Carbohydrates:	31 g
Fiber:	2 g
Sugars:	3 g
Protein:	33 g

It used to be that you had to visit an Asian market to find bok choy, but as America has gone "greener" you'll find this member of the healthful brassica family in most well-stocked produce sections. It's rich in vitamins A and C, and its mild flavor plays well here with the rich taste of the grilled turkey and peanut sauce. Look for peanut sauce in the international aisle of your local grocer.

INGREDIENTS

8 oz. 97% fat-free ground white turkey

1/2 tsp. salt ground

Black pepper to taste

1 c. chopped bok choy

1 4"×4" whole wheat ciabatta roll

1 tbsp. peanut sauce

DIRECTIONS

Preheat gas or charcoal grill according to manufacturer's directions, or heat small grill pan over medium heat.

In a small bowl, combine ground turkey, salt and pepper to taste. Divide evenly into fourths and shape four burgers.

Place burger on grill and cook for approximately 5-6 minutes on each side or until completely cooked through.

While burger is grilling, spray small sauté pan with cooking spray and set over medium-high heat. Add bok choy to hot pan, season with 1/4 teaspoon salt and pepper to taste, and cook until greens are reduced in size and softened, approximately 2-3 minutes. Remove pan from heat once bok choy is cooked. Split ciabatta in half horizontally and spread peanut sauce on each half. Then place bok choy and turkey burger on one ciabatta half, cover with remaining ciabatta half, and cut in half to serve.

Prep time:	6 min.
Cook time:	12 min.
Total time:	18 min.
Yield:	2 servings
Serving size:	1/2 burger

TOTAL TIME **18** min.

DINNER

END EVERY DAY DELICIOUSLY

Spicy Chickpea Patty
with Cilantro Lime & Green Chilies

NUTRITIONAL INFORMATION
Per Serving

Calories:	287
Total Fat:	3 g
Cholesterol:	31 mg
Sodium:	808 mg
Total Carbohydrates:	53 g
Fiber:	10 g
Sugars:	11 g
Protein:	12 g

Chickpeas are staples of Mediterranean cuisine, but we like the way their nutty taste marries with Latin American flavors. A large green salad is just the right accompaniment to these protein-and fiber-rich patties.

INGREDIENTS

3 15-oz. cans chickpeas, drained
1 large egg
1/4 c. fresh salsa
1 tbsp. fresh lime juice
  (approx. 1/2 lime)
1/4 c. finely chopped Anaheim
  chile, seeds removed
1/4 c. corn flake crumbs
1 tbsp. chopped fresh cilantro
1/4 tsp. salt
1/8 tsp. ground cayenne pepper
1/8 tsp. ground black pepper
1/2 tsp. vegetable oil

DIRECTIONS

In work bowl of food processor, grind chickpeas into a chunky paste for 15 seconds or 5 pulses, scraping sides of bowl down between pulses. Place processed chickpeas into large mixing bowl and combine with remaining ingredients; mix well with spatula. Cover bowl with plastic wrap and refrigerate for 45 minutes.

Adjust oven rack to upper-middle position and heat oven to 350 degrees. Line rimmed baking sheet with foil. Remove chickpea mixture from refrigerator. Use 2-ounce dough scoop or your hands to portion out golf-ball-sized pieces; shape into patties.

Place vegetable oil in 10-inch non stick sauté pan. With paper towel, spread oil over surface of pan, then wipe away excess. Place pan over medium-high heat, then put patties in pan and cook until golden brown, approximately 2 minutes per side. Remove sautéed patties from pan and place on lined baking sheet. Bake for 15 minutes.

Prep time:	10 min.
Cook time:	17 min.
Total time:	27 min.
Yield:	6 servings
Serving size:	2 patties

TOTAL TIME 27 min.

TOTAL TIME 23 min.

Pan Seared Tofu with Spicy Orange Sauce

Even meat-eaters like this spicy-sweet, meatless meal!

INGREDIENTS

1 14-oz. package extra firm tofu, drained and pressed of excess moisture*

1/2 tsp. salt

1/4 tsp. ground black pepper

1 tbsp. extra virgin olive oil

* Drain water from package of tofu, then wrap tofu block in several paper towel sheets. Place a heavy pan or a large can of tomatoes on wrapped tofu for at least 10 minutes and preferably 30 minutes to press out excess water.

DIRECTIONS

Cut tofu into four pieces lengthwise. Place 10-inch skillet over medium-high heat. Add extra virgin olive oil to skillet. When oil begins to shimmer, add tofu slices. Cook tofu 4 minutes per side, until golden brown. Remove cooked tofu from pan and drizzle 3 tablespoons Spicy Orange Sauce (recipe follows) over each tofu steak before serving.

Prep time:	15 min.
Cook time:	8 min.
Total time:	23 min.
Yield:	4 servings
Serving size:	1 tofu steak & 3 tbsp. sauce

INGREDIENTS Spicy Orange Sauce

1/2 c. orange juice

1/4 cup white wine

1/8 tsp. ground cayenne pepper

1/8 tsp. hot pepper sauce

1/8 tsp. vegetable bouillon base

1/2 tsp. cornstarch

1 tsp. Smart Balance Buttery Spread

1/8 tsp. salt

Dash ground black pepper

DIRECTIONS

In medium-sized saucepan combine all ingredients except Smart Balance spread. Bring to boil, stirring constantly with whisk, and boil for 2 minutes. Remove pan from heat and add Smart Balance spread; use whisk to stir and blend spread into sauce.

Prep time:	0 min.
Cook time:	5 min.
Total time:	5 min.
Yield:	3/4 c.
Serving size:	3 tbsp.

NUTRITIONAL INFORMATION
Per Serving

Calories:	128
Total Fat:	9 g
Cholesterol:	3 mg
Sodium:	334 mg
Total Carbohydrates:	3 g
Fiber:	0 g
Sugars:	1 g
Protein:	10 g

Spicy Orange Sauce
NUTRITIONAL INFORMATION
Per Serving

Calories:	29
Total Fat:	0 g
Cholesterol:	0 mg
Sodium:	140 mg
Total Carbohydrates:	4 g
Fiber:	0 g
Sugars:	3 g
Protein:	0 g

Turkey Sage & Pine Nut Meatballs

NUTRITIONAL INFORMATION
Per Serving

Calories:	136
Total Fat:	3 g
Cholesterol:	83 mg
Sodium:	184 mg
Total Carbohydrates:	7 g
Fiber:	0 g
Sugars:	0 g
Protein:	24 g

Are these meatballs like your Nana used to make? Not exactly, but we think she'd approve of this tasty version. You can freeze leftover cooked meatballs, or add them to a fat-free tomato sauce for another meal.

INGREDIENTS

1 1/4 lb. 97% fat-free ground white turkey
1/3 c. pine nuts
1 tbsp. chopped fresh sage
1 tsp. minced garlic
1 tbsp. finely chopped onion
1/4 tsp. salt
1/8 tsp. ground black pepper
1 large egg
1/4 c. corn flake crumbs

DIRECTIONS

In large mixing bowl, combine all ingredients and mix well by hand. Cover bowl with plastic wrap and refrigerate for 1 hour.

Adjust oven rack to upper-middle position and heat oven to 350 degrees. Line rimmed baking sheet with foil and set aside.

Use 2-ounce dough scoop or your hands to portion out 10 golf ball-sized pieces; shape into meatballs and place on rimmed baking sheet. Bake for 20 minutes or until meatballs are browned and cooked through.

Prep time:	10 min.
Cook time:	20 min.
Total time:	30 min.
Yield:	6 servings
Serving size:	2 meatballs

TOTAL TIME 30 min.

TOTAL TIME **32** min.

Turkey Chili Con Carne

The flavor of this chili gets even better after a night in the fridge. Make it for a late Sunday night dinner, then enjoy leftovers for lunch that week. You can also freeze leftovers in small containers for impromptu meals.

Look for dried ancho chiles in your grocer's produce section.

INGREDIENTS

1   tbsp. extra virgin olive oil
2   lbs. 97% fat-free ground white turkey
1   tsp. Mexican-style seasoning
1/2 tsp. fresh oregano, chopped
1/2 tsp. salt
1/4 tsp. ground black pepper
2   c. tomato sauce
1   c. canned pinto beans in chili sauce
1/2 c. water
1   dried ancho chile
1   tsp. hot pepper sauce
1/8 tsp. ground cayenne pepper

DIRECTIONS

Set 10-inch sauté pan over medium-high heat and add olive oil to pan. When oil begins to shimmer, add ground turkey; use spatula to break turkey into small pieces and cook until evenly browned, about 5 minutes. Use large spoon to remove fat from pan (tilt pan to make this easier). Stir in Mexican seasoning, oregano, salt and pepper, and cook 4 to 6 minutes longer. Reduce heat and add remaining ingredients; simmer for 15-20 minutes, adding more water if chili looks too thick. Remove ancho chile before serving.

Prep time:	2 min.
Cook time:	30 min.
Total time:	32 min.
Yield:	10 servings
Serving size:	1/2 cup

NUTRITIONAL INFORMATION
Per Serving

Calories:	202
Total Fat:	9 g
Cholesterol:	64 mg
Sodium:	1044 mg
Total Carbohydrates:	12 g
Fiber:	3 g
Sugars:	6 g
Protein:	21 g

Grilled Jumbo Shrimp
with Lemon Pepper Garlic Sauce

NUTRITIONAL INFORMATION
Per Serving

Calories:	121
Total Fat:	2 g
Cholesterol:	165 mg
Sodium:	490 mg
Total Carbohydrates:	5 g
Fiber:	0 g
Sugars:	2 g
Protein:	18 g

Lemon Pepper Sauce
NUTRITIONAL INFORMATION
Per Serving

Calories:	41
Total Fat:	1 g
Cholesterol:	0 mg
Sodium:	177 mg
Total Carbohydrates:	5 g
Fiber:	0 g
Sugars:	2 g
Protein:	0 g

Often, shrimp is served with heavy sauces that mask the flavor and freshness of the shrimp itself. The beauty of this recipe is that the sauce is light and delicate and only serves to enhance the shrimp's subtle yet delicious flavor.

INGREDIENTS

16 16/20 count shrimp, tail-on, peeled and deveined

1/4 tsp. kosher salt

1/4 tsp. ground black pepper

4 wooden skewers, soaked in water for 20 minutes

1/2 c. Lemon Pepper Sauce (recipe follows)

DIRECTIONS

Preheat grill according to manufacturer's directions or set grill pan over medium-high heat. Thread four pieces of shrimp on each skewer and season with salt and pepper. Grill shrimp 2-3 minutes per side. Serve shrimp off the skewer with 2 tablespoons Lemon Pepper Sauce (recipe follows) per serving.

Prep time:	5 min.
Cook time:	6 min.
Total time:	11 min.
Yield:	4 servings
Serving size:	4 shrimp

INGREDIENTS Lemon Pepper Garlic Sauc

1/2 c. low-sodium chicken broth

1/4 c. lemon juice

1/4 c. white wine

2 tbsp. Worcestershire sauce

1 tbsp. minced garlic

1/8 tsp. kosher salt

2 tsp. coarsely ground black pepper

1/2 tsp. cornstarch

1 tsp. Smart Balance Buttery Spread

DIRECTIONS

In medium-sized saucepan, combine all ingredients except Smart Balance spread over medium-high heat. Bring to boil, stirring constantly with whisk, for 2 minutes. Remove pan from heat and whisk in Smart Balance spread until blended into sauce. Allow to sit for 5 minutes before serving.

Prep time:	0 min.
Cook time:	5 min.
Total time:	5 min.
Yield:	1 c.
Serving size:	2 tbsp. sauce

TOTAL TIME **11** min.

TOTAL TIME 25 min.

Fillet of Halibut with Spicy Orange Sauce

The halibut is a fish well worth its (sea) salt. The firm white meat and delicate sweet flavor make it a favorite among fish lovers.

Many sauces contain high calories and sugars. While our sauces are already a healthier alternative, you still need to watch how much of it you drizzle over your own serving. Two tablespoons of sauce is more than enough to let you enjoy all the aromatic flavors without costing you too many calories.

INGREDIENTS

4 4-oz. halibut filets

1 tbsp. extra-virgin olive oil

1/2 tsp. kosher salt

1/4 tsp. ground black pepper

1/2 c. Spicy Orange Sauce (recipe follows)

DIRECTIONS

Adjust oven rack to upper-middle position and heat oven to 350 degrees. Line rimmed baking sheet with foil.

Coat each halibut fillet with oil and season with salt and pepper. Place filets on baking sheet and bake for 15-20 minutes, or until just cooked through. Drizzle each filet with 2 tablespoons Spicy Orange Sauce (recipe follows) before serving.

Prep time: 5 min.
Cook time: 20 min.
Total time: 25 min.
Yield: 4 servings
Serving size: 1 halibut fillet

INGREDIENTS Spicy Orange Sauce

1/2 c. orange juice

1/4 c. white wine

1/8 tsp. ground cayenne pepper

1/8 tsp. hot pepper sauce

1/8 tsp. vegetable bouillon base

1/2 tsp. cornstarch

1 tsp. Smart Balance Buttery Spread

1/8 tsp. salt

Dash ground black pepper

DIRECTIONS

In medium-sized saucepan combine all ingredients except Smart Balance spread. Bring to boil, stirring constantly with whisk, and boil for 2 minutes. Remove pan from heat and add Smart Balance spread; use whisk to stir and blend spread into sauce.

Prep time: 0 min.
Cook time: 5 min.
Total time: 5 min.
Yield: 3/4 c.
Serving size: 2 tbsp.

NUTRITIONAL INFORMATION
Per Serving

Calories:	218
Total Fat:	7 g
Cholesterol:	49 mg
Sodium:	463 mg
Total Carbohydrates:	4 g
Fiber:	0 g
Sugars:	2 g
Protein:	30 g

Spicy Orange Sauce
NUTRITIONAL INFORMATION
Per Serving

Calories:	29
Total Fat:	0 g
Cholesterol:	0 mg
Sodium:	140 mg
Total Carbohydrates:	4 g
Fiber:	0 g
Sugars:	3 g
Protein:	0 g

Pan Seared Sea Scallops with Ginger Jerk Sauce

Scallops are a very popular and delicious shellfish, even among those who are not particularly fond of fish or other shellfish.

The secret to successful scallop cooking is to not overcook them because that makes them tough. Before placing the scallops inside, make sure the oil is very hot. That way you will get a good sear on each side without overcooking them.

NUTRITIONAL INFORMATION
Per Serving

Calories:	201
Total Fat:	5 g
Cholesterol:	62 mg
Sodium:	714 mg
Total Carbohydrates:	10 g
Fiber:	0 g
Sugars:	6 g
Protein:	27 g

Ginger Jerk Sauce

NUTRITIONAL INFORMATION
Per Serving

Calories:	44
Total Fat:	0 g
Cholesterol:	0 mg
Sodium:	290 mg
Total Carbohydrates:	10 g
Fiber:	0 g
Sugars:	6 g
Protein:	1 g

INGREDIENTS

12 large sea scallops
1/4 tsp. kosher salt
1/4 tsp. ground black pepper
1 tbsp. extra-virgin olive oil
1/2 c. Ginger Jerk Sauce
   (recipe follows)

DIRECTIONS

Pat scallops dry and season with salt and pepper. Heat half the oil in a 12-inch nonstick skillet over medium-high heat until oil is very hot, but not smoking. Add six scallops to the pan, and sear until golden brown, 1 to 2 minutes per side. Transfer seared scallops to a platter and repeat with remaining oil and scallops. Divide scallops between four dinner plates and serve each with 2 tablespoons Ginger Jerk Sauce (recipe follows).

Prep time:	5 min.
Cook time:	4 min.
Total time:	9 min.
Yield:	4 servings
Serving size:	3 scallops

INGREDIENTS Ginger Jerk Sauce

1/2 c. pineapple juice
1/4 c. apple cider vinegar
2 tbsp. lower-sodium soy sauce
1 tbsp. light brown sugar
2 tbsp. fresh grated ginger
1 tbsp. minced garlic
1 tbsp. fresh thyme
1 tsp. ground allspice
1/2 tsp. pumpkin pie spice
1/2 tsp. cayenne pepper
1/2 tsp. cornstarch

DIRECTIONS

Combine all the ingredients in a small saucepan over medium-high heat and bring to boil. Reduce heat and simmer for 3-5 minutes. Serve with Seared Scallops.

Prep time:	0 min.
Cook time:	7 min.
Total time:	7 min.
Yield:	3/4 c.
Serving size:	2 tbsp.

TOTAL TIME 9 min.

TOTAL TIME **17** min.

Fillet of Salmon with Spiced Pomegranate Sauce

The richness of the salmon provides the right foil for the piquant flavor of the pomegranate sauce. They should spring back when you press your finger into them, a sign of freshness.

This recipe calls for Chinese five spice powder, which is a blend of star anise, cloves, cinnamon, Sichuan pepper and fennel.

INGREDIENTS

6 4-oz. salmon fillets
1/2 tsp. salt
1/4 tsp. ground black pepper

DIRECTIONS

Adjust oven rack to upper-middle position and heat oven to 350 degrees. Line rimmed baking sheet with foil.

Season salmon fillets with salt and pepper and place skin-side down on baking sheet. Bake for 10-12 minutes until just cooked through. Drizzle two tablespoons of Spicy Pomegranate Sauce (recipe follows) over each fillet before serving.

Prep time:	5 min.
Cook time:	12 min.
Total time:	17 min.
Yield:	6 servings
Serving size:	1 salmon filet

INGREDIENTS Spicy Pomegranate Sauce

1 c. bottled pomegranate juice
1/4 c. honey
1 tsp. lemon juice
1 tbsp. water
1 tsp. cornstarch
1/4 tsp. salt
1/4 tsp. ground black pepper
1/4 tsp. ground cinnamon
1/4 tsp. ground coriander
1/8 tsp. ground ginger
1/8 tsp. ground cayenne pepper
1/8 tsp. Chinese five spice powder
1 tbsp. Smart Balance Buttery Spread

DIRECTIONS

In small saucepan, combine all ingredients except Smart Balance Spread. Bring to boil, then reduce heat to low and simmer for 10 min. Remove pan from heat. Add Smart Balance Spread and whisk until blended into sauce.

Prep time:	0 min.
Cook time:	10 min.
Total time:	10 min.
Yield:	1 1/4 c.
Serving size:	2 tbsp.

**NUTRITIONAL INFORMATION
Per Serving**

Calories:	279
Total Fat:	13 g
Cholesterol:	57 mg
Sodium:	362 mg
Total Carbohydrates:	18 g
Fiber:	0 g
Sugars:	17 g
Protein:	23 g

Spicy Pomegranate Sauce
**NUTRITIONAL INFORMATION
Per Serving**

Calories:	76
Total Fat:	1 g
Cholesterol:	0 mg
Sodium:	115 mg
Total Carbohydrates:	18 g
Fiber:	0 g
Sugars:	17 g
Protein:	0 g

Fillet of Cod with Orange Tea Leaf Sauce

NUTRITIONAL INFORMATION
Per Serving

Calories:	180
Total Fat:	4 g
Cholesterol:	55 mg
Sodium:	474 mg
Total Carbohydrates:	5 g
Fiber:	0 g
Sugars:	4 g
Protein:	26 g

Orange Tea Leaf Sauce
NUTRITIONAL INFORMATION
Per Serving

Calories:	30
Total Fat:	0 g
Cholesterol:	0 mg
Sodium:	124 mg
Total Carbohydrates:	5 g
Fiber:	0 g
Sugars:	4 g
Protein:	0 g

Fish, specifically cod, promotes cardiovascular health because it is a good source of blood-thinning omega-3 fatty acids. Other healthy components in this dish include black tea, which recent studies have linked to weight loss, and orange, which supplies nearly 100 percent of the recommended daily dietary intake of vitamin C.

Even though fish is healthy and diet friendly, most people don't eat it as often as they should. The recommended amount of fish is two to three times a week.

INGREDIENTS

4 4-oz. cod fillets
1 tbsp. extra-virgin olive oil
1/2 tsp. kosher salt
1/4 tsp. ground black pepper
1/2 c. Orange Tea Leaf Sauce
   (recipe follows)

DIRECTIONS

Adjust oven rack to upper-middle position and heat oven to 350 degrees. Line rimmed baking sheet with foil.

Coat each cod fillet with oil and season with salt and pepper. Place fillets on baking sheet and bake for 15-20 minutes, or until just cooked through. Drizzle each fillet with two tablespoons Orange Tea Leaf Sauce (recipe follows) before serving.

Prep time:	5 min.
Cook time:	20 min.
Total time:	25 min.
Yield:	4 servings
Serving size:	1 cod fillet

INGREDIENTS Orange Tea Leaf Sauce

1/4 c. water
1/2 c. orange juice
1 black tea bag
1/4 c. white wine
1 tsp. light brown sugar
1/4 tsp. kosher salt
1/8 ground black pepper
1/4 tsp. cornstarch

DIRECTIONS

Heat up water and orange juice in a small saucepan over medium heat. Take pan off the heat, add the tea bag and let it steep for 5 minutes. Discard tea bag, place saucepan back over medium heat, whisk in remaining ingredients and bring to a boil. Lower heat and simmer until sauce has thickened, stirring frequently, about 3-5 minutes. Remove pan from heat and allow to sit for 5 minutes before serving.

Prep time:	5 min.
Cook time:	8 min.
Total time:	13 min.
Yield:	3/4 c.
Serving size:	2 tbsp.

Basil Pesto Sole Roulade

Here's an elegant — and easy! — way to serve fish for dinner tonight. If you can't find pine nuts at your local grocer, substitute walnuts or almonds. Pressed for time? Substitute a store-bought pesto for homemade.

INGREDIENTS

4 4-oz. sole fillets
1/2 tsp. salt
1/4 tsp. ground black pepper
2 c. chopped fresh basil
1/2 c. extra virgin olive oil
1/4 c. pine nuts
1/4 c. grated Parmesan cheese
1 medium garlic clove
Cooking spray

DIRECTIONS

Adjust oven rack to upper middle position and heat oven to 400 degrees. Spray rimmed baking sheet with cooking spray, and place sole fillets on sheet. Season with salt and pepper and set aside.

Place basil and 1 tablespoon of olive oil in work bowl of food processor or in blender jar, then process or blend into paste. Add pine nuts, cheese and garlic. Then while running processor/blender, add remaining olive oil in slow, steady stream through lid opening; process or blend until pesto is smooth, about 1 minute.

Divide pesto among four fillets, placing one spoonful on bottom of each fillet. Roll each fillet and place seam-side down on baking sheet. (Insert toothpick through fillet to help keep it rolled.) Bake for 15 minutes or until fillets are opaque and cooked through.

Prep time:	15 min.
Cook time:	15 min.
Total time:	30 min.
Yield:	4 servings
Serving size:	1 roulade

NUTRITIONAL INFORMATION
Per Serving

Calories:	415
Total Fat:	37 g
Cholesterol:	77 mg
Sodium:	457 mg
Total Carbohydrates:	2 g
Fiber:	1 g
Sugars:	0 g
Protein:	23 g

Roasted Pork Loin with Apricot Curry Sauce

NUTRITIONAL INFORMATION
Per Serving

Calories:	182
Total Fat:	4 g
Cholesterol:	60 mg
Sodium:	720 mg
Total Carbohydrates:	5 g
Fiber:	1 g
Sugars:	4 g
Protein:	28 g

Apricot Curry Sauce
NUTRITIONAL INFORMATION
Per Serving

Calories:	42
Total Fat:	1 g
Cholesterol:	1 mg
Sodium:	75 mg
Total Carbohydrates:	5 g
Fiber:	1 g
Sugars:	4 g
Protein:	1 g

Pork loin is a mildly flavored cut, which means it pairs well with a vibrant sauce like this South Asian-inspired one. Boneless pork loin usually is sold in a 3- to 4-pound roast, so ask your butcher to cut it down to the size you need. You can also wrap and freeze the rest for future meals.

INGREDIENTS
1 lb. boneless pork loin
1 tsp. salt
1/4 tsp. ground black pepper

DIRECTIONS
Adjust oven rack to upper-middle position and heat oven to 375 degrees. Line rimmed baking sheet with foil and place roasting rack on sheet.

Rub pork loin with salt and pepper. Roast for 20-25 minutes until internal temperature of roast measures 150 degrees. Rest loin on roasting rack for 10 minutes before cutting into 3/4-inch slices. Drizzle each serving with two tablespoons of Apricot Curry Sauce (recipe follows) before serving.

Prep time:	5 min.
Cook time:	25 min.
Total time:	30 min.
Yield:	4 servings
Serving size:	4 oz. pork loin

INGREDIENTS Apricot Curry Sauce
1 tsp. extra virgin olive oil
4 fresh apricots, pitted and chopped into 1/2" pieces
1/4 c. white wine
1/2 tsp. curry powder
1/2 tsp. light brown sugar
1/8 tsp. salt
1/2 c. water
1/4 tsp. cornstarch

DIRECTIONS
Heat oil in a small saucepan over medium heat. Add apricots, and sauté until tender, 5-7 minutes. Stir in wine, curry powder, brown sugar and salt, reduce heat, and simmer for 10 minutes. Whisk water and cornstarch together in a small bowl until smooth. Add to saucepan and cook until thickened, about 5 minutes. If a smoother consistency is desired, puree sauce in a blender before serving.

Prep time:	5 min.
Cook time:	25 min.
Total time:	30 min.
Yield:	3 /4 c.
Serving size:	2 tbsp.

TOTAL TIME 30 min.

TOTAL TIME 15 min.

New York Strip Steak with Mango BBQ Sauce

Red meat may have a bad rap in the health industry, but if eaten in moderation, it can actually be good for you. Red meat provides high levels of vital nutrients, including iron. With its South American slant, our New York Strip Steak with Mango BBQ Sauce really pops with flavor!

INGREDIENTS

1 12-oz. New York strip steak
1 tbsp. extra-virgin olive oil
1/2 tsp. kosher salt
1/4 tsp. ground black pepper
1/2 c. Mango BBQ Sauce (recipe follows)

DIRECTIONS

Preheat grill according to manufacturer's directions.

Pat steak dry with paper towels and season with salt and pepper. When fire is hot, place steak on lightly oiled grill rack; grill for approximately 5 minutes per side for medium rare. Remove steak to cutting board and allow to rest for 10 minutes. Slice steak into 1/2-inch wide strips, slicing across the grain on a slight angle. Divide steak between four plates and serve each with 2 table-spoons Mango BBQ Sauce.

Prep time: 5 min.
Cook time: 10 min.
Total time: 15 min.
Yield: 4 servings
Serving size: 4 oz. steak

INGREDIENTS Mango BBQ Sauce

1/3 c. ketchup
1/3 c. mango puree
2 tbsp. apple cider vinegar
1/2 tbsp. light brown sugar
1 tsp. Dijon mustard
1/8 tsp. kosher salt
1/8 tsp. ground black pepper
1/8 tsp. cayenne pepper

DIRECTIONS

Combine all the ingredients in a small saucepan over medium-high heat and bring to boil. Reduce heat and simmer for 3-5 minutes. Serve with Grilled Strip Steak.

Prep time: 0 min.
Cook time: 8 min.
Total time: 8 min.
Yield: 2/3 c.
Serving size: 2 tbsp.

NUTRITIONAL INFORMATION
Per Serving

Calories:	239
Total Fat:	9 g
Cholesterol:	60 mg
Sodium:	587 mg
Total Carbohydrates:	10 g
Fiber:	0 g
Sugars:	5 g
Protein:	28 g

Mango BBQ Sauce
NUTRITIONAL INFORMATION
Per Serving

Calories:	41
Total Fat:	0 g
Cholesterol:	0 mg
Sodium:	292 mg
Total Carbohydrates:	10 g
Fiber:	0 g
Sugars:	5 g
Protein:	0 g

Grilled London Broil with Raspberry Chipotle Sauce

NUTRITIONAL INFORMATION
Per Serving

Calories:	286
Total Fat:	12 g
Cholesterol:	63 mg
Sodium:	328 mg
Total Carbohydrates:	2 g
Fiber:	0 g
Sugars:	1 g
Protein:	36 g

Raspberry Chipotle Sauce
NUTRITIONAL INFORMATION
Per Serving

Calories:	26
Total Fat:	1 g
Cholesterol:	0 mg
Sodium:	59 mg
Total Carbohydrates:	2 g
Fiber:	0 g
Sugars:	1 g
Protein:	0 g

Flank steak is flavorful and fairly easy to prepare – the trick is to not overcook it on the grill. This lean cut should be cooked to an internal temperature of 140 degrees; the resting period will keep the steak tender and juicy.

INGREDIENTS
1 1/2 lb. flank steak
1/2 tsp. salt
1/4 tsp. ground black pepper

DIRECTIONS
Preheat grill according to manufacturer's directions.
Season steak with salt and pepper. Grill steak for approximately 4-6 minutes for medium rare (7-8 minutes for medium), then flip over to grill for another 4-6 minutes (7-8 minutes for medium). Remove steak to cutting board; allow to rest for 5-7 minutes before slicing into 1/2-inch wide strips cut at 45-degree angle. Serve with two tablespoons Raspberry Chipotle Sauce per serving (recipe follows).

Prep time:	5 min.
Cook time:	12 min.
Total time:	17 min.
Yield:	6 servings
Serving size:	4 oz. steak

INGREDIENTS Raspberry Chipotle Sauce
1 canned chipotle chile in adobo sauce
8 fresh raspberries
1/4 tsp. vegetable bouillon base
1/2 c. white wine
1/4 c. water
1 tsp. light brown sugar
1/2 tsp. cornstarch
1 tsp. Smart Balance Buttery Spread

DIRECTIONS
In small saucepan, combine all ingredients except Smart Balance Spread and bring to boil, stirring frequently to incorporate cornstarch. Reduce heat to low and simmer for 4-5 minutes, then remove pan from heat. Remove chipotle chile from sauce and discard. Add Smart Balance Spread and whisk until blended into sauce.

Prep time:	0 min.
Cook time:	8 min.
Total time:	8 min.
Yield:	3/4 c.
Serving size:	2 tbsp.

TOTAL TIME 17 min.

TOTAL TIME **35** min.

Stuffed Chicken Breast with Apples and Almonds

Throughout history it was believed that eating fruit with meat would aid in digestion, and science has proven this true. Moreover, the combination of apple and chicken is simply delicious. The sliced almonds lend a satisfying crunch to the finished dish.

INGREDIENTS

4 4-oz. chicken breast fillets
1 Granny Smith apple, peeled, cored, and cut into 8 wedges
1/4 c. sliced blanched almonds
1/2 tsp. salt
1/4 tsp. ground black pepper
Cooking spray

DIRECTIONS

Adjust oven rack to upper-middle position and heat oven to 350 degrees. Line rimmed baking sheet with foil and spray with cooking spray.

Place chicken fillets on cutting board. Use your palm to hold fillet down flat on board, then take sharp knife and cut fillet in half horizontally, stopping about 1/4-inch from edge. Open up cut chicken fillet (will resemble a butterfly), and place between two sheets wax paper. Using meat mallet, pound fillet until even and thin, about 1/4-inch thick. Repeat with remaining fillets. Season chicken with salt and pepper.

Place two wedges of apple in center of fillet, then top with 1/4 of almonds. Roll chicken from bottom to top, and place seam-side down on baking sheet. Repeat with remaining fillets. Bake for 15-20 minutes until chicken is thoroughly cooked.

Prep time:	15 min.
Cook time:	20 min.
Total time:	35 min.
Yield:	4 chicken fillets
Serves:	4 servings
Serving size:	1 stuffed breast

NUTRITIONAL INFORMATION
Per Serving

Calories:	218
Total Fat:	9 g
Cholesterol:	73 mg
Sodium:	423 mg
Total Carbohydrates:	9 g
Fiber:	2 g
Sugars:	5 g
Protein:	26 g

Walnut Crusted Apricot Chicken Roulade

NUTRITIONAL INFORMATION
Per Serving

Calories:	264
Total Fat:	13 g
Cholesterol:	73 mg
Sodium:	459 mg
Total Carbohydrates:	9 g
Fiber:	1 g
Sugars:	2 g
Protein:	28 g

If you spot fresh apricots for sale at a farmer's market, grab them! These highly perishable stone fruits are best enjoyed in June and July. They're extra yummy when paired with chicken.

INGREDIENTS

4 4-oz. chicken breast fillets

2 apricots, pitted and cut into
 4 pieces

1/2 tsp. salt

1/4 tsp. ground black pepper

1/2 c. walnuts, toasted
 and finely chopped

1/2 c. panko breadcrumbs

1 egg white, beaten

Cooking spray

DIRECTIONS

Adjust oven rack to upper-middle position and heat oven to 350 degrees. Line rimmed baking sheet with foil and spray with cooking spray. Put chicken fillets on cutting board. Using your palm to hold fillet down flat on board, take sharp knife and cut fillet in half horizontally, stopping about 1/4-inch from edge. Open cut fillet (will resemble butterfly) and put between two sheets of wax paper. Using meat mallet pound fillet until even and thin, about 1/4-inch thick. Repeat with remaining fillets. Sprinkle chicken fillets with salt and pepper. Place

1/4 of chopped apricots in center of fillet and roll fillet from bottom to top.

Combine walnuts and breadcrumbs in a shallow dish, and place egg whites in another shallow dish. Roll each prepared roulade in the beaten egg white, and then into the walnut mixture. Place seam-side down on baking sheet. Bake for 15-20 minutes until cooked through. Remove fillets to cutting board. Let rest for 5-7 minutes before cutting into 1-inch wide slices for serving

Prep time:	20 min.
Cook time:	20 min.
Total time:	40 min.
Yield:	4 servings
Serving size:	1 roulade

Steamed Broccolini

INGREDIENTS

1 lb. broccolini, ends trimmed

1/4 tsp. kosher salt

1/4 tsp. ground black pepper

DIRECTIONS

In a steamer set over boiling water, steam broccolini, covered, until crisp tender, 6-7 minutes. Season with salt and pepper, and serve.

NUTRITIONAL INFORMATION
Per Serving

Calories:	25
Total Fat:	0.8 g
Cholesterol:	0 mg
Sodium:	131 mg
Total Carbohydrates:	4 g
Fiber:	2.8 g
Sugars:	1 g
Protein:	1 g

Prep time:	5 min.
Cook time:	10 min.
Total time:	15 min.
Yield:	4 servings
Serving size:	1/2 c.

Sesame Baby Bok Choy

INGREDIENTS

1 tbsp. salad oil
(75% canola oil, 25% olive oil)

1 lb. baby bok choy ends trimmed and halved

2 tbsp. less sodium soy sauce

1 tbsp. toasted sesame seeds

1/4 tsp. ground black pepper

DIRECTIONS

Heat oil in a 12-inch skillet over medium-high heat. Add bok choy and soy sauce, and cook 3-5 minutes, until greens are wilted and stalks are crisp tender. Stir in sesame seeds and black pepper, and serve.

NUTRITIONAL INFORMATION
Per Serving

Calories:	58
Total Fat:	4.3 g
Cholesterol:	0 mg
Sodium:	374 mg
Total Carbohydrates:	3.6 g
Fiber:	1 g
Sugars:	1.5 g
Protein:	2 g

Prep time:	5 min
Cook time:	5 min
Total time:	10 min
Yield:	4 servings
Serving size:	1/2 c.

Zucchini Rounds Stewed in Fresh Marinara Sauce

INGREDIENTS

- 2 tbsp. extra-virgin olive oil
- 2 medium zucchini, sliced into 1/2" rounds
- 1 c. marinara sauce
- 1/4 tsp. ground black pepper

DIRECTIONS

Heat oil in a 12-inch nonstick skillet over medium-high heat. Add zucchini, and sauté until tender, about 5 minutes. Stir in marinara sauce, bring to a simmer, and cook for an additional 5 minutes. Season with black pepper and serve.

NUTRITIONAL INFORMATION
Per Serving

Calories:	124
Total Fat:	9.7 g
Cholesterol:	5 mg
Sodium:	223 mg
Total Carbohydrates:	8.7 g
Fiber:	0 g
Sugars:	2 g
Protein:	2 g

Prep time:	5 min.
Cook time:	10 min.
Total time:	15 min.
Yield:	4 servings
Serving size:	1/2 c.

Green Beans with Walnuts & Garlic

INGREDIENTS

- 1 lb. green beans cut into 2" lengths
- 1 tbsp. extra-virgin olive oil
- 4 cloves garlic, sliced thin
- 1/2 c. chopped toasted walnuts
- 1/4 tsp. kosher salt
- 1/4 tsp. ground black pepper

DIRECTIONS

In a large pot of boiling salted water, blanch* the green beans for 3 minutes; drain and pat dry. Combine oil and garlic in a 12-inch skillet over medium heat; cook until softened, about 5 minutes. Add the blanched beans, and sauté until heated through. Stir in the walnuts, season with salt and pepper, and serve.

NUTRITIONAL INFORMATION
Per Serving

Calories:	171
Total Fat:	13 g
Cholesterol:	2.5 mg
Sodium:	124 mg
Total Carbohydrates:	11.5 g
Fiber:	4.7 g
Sugars:	2 g
Protein:	6 g

Prep time:	10 min.
Cook time:	20 min.
Total time:	30 min.
Yield:	4 servings
Serving size:	1/2 c.

*Blanching: A vegetable is plunged into boiling water for a brief moment, then plunged into ice water to stop the cooking process.

Grilled Yellow Tomato

INGREDIENTS

2 large yellow tomatoes, quartered and seeds removed

1 tbsp. extra-virgin olive oil

1/4 tsp. kosher salt

1/4 tsp. ground black pepper

DIRECTIONS

Preheat grill according to manufacturer's directions or set grill pan over medium-high heat.

Toss tomatoes with oil, salt and pepper in a large bowl. Brush grill rack with oil, and grill tomatoes until blistered and charred, turning occasionally, about 6 minutes.

NUTRITIONAL INFORMATION
Per Serving

Calories:	46
Total Fat:	3.7 g
Cholesterol:	2.5 mg
Sodium:	147 mg
Total Carbohydrates:	3 g
Fiber:	0 g
Sugars:	0 g
Protein:	1 g

Prep time:	5 min.
Cook time:	6 min.
Total time:	11 min.
Yield:	4 servings
Serving size:	2 tomate quarters

Roasted Lemon Parsley Brussels Sprouts

INGREDIENTS

1 lb. Brussels sprouts, trimmed and halved lengthwise

1 tbsp. extra-virgin olive oil

1/2 tsp. kosher salt

1/4 tsp. ground black pepper

1 lemon, zested

2 tbsp. minced parsley

DIRECTIONS

Preheat oven to 400 degrees. Place Brussels sprouts on a rimmed baking sheet, and toss with oil, salt and pepper. Spread brussles sprouts out, and roast stirring once, until deep golden brown, 30-35 minutes. Transfer to a large bowl, and toss with lemon zest and parsley.

NUTRITIONAL INFORMATION
Per Serving

Calories:	86
Total Fat:	3.8 g
Cholesterol:	2.5 mg
Sodium:	275 mg
Total Carbohydrates:	10 g
Fiber:	4.5 g
Sugars:	2.5 g
Protein:	4 g

Prep time:	10 min
Cook time:	35 min
Total time:	45 min
Yield:	4 servings
Serving size:	3/4 c.

Roasted Artichoke Hearts

INGREDIENTS

2 14 oz. cans artichoke hearts,
    drained and rinsed

1 tbsp. extra-virgin olive oil

1/4 tsp. kosher salt

1/4 tsp. ground black pepper

DIRECTIONS

Preheat oven to 375 degrees. Place artichoke hearts on a rimmed baking sheet, and toss with oil, salt and pepper. Spread artichoke hearts out, and roast stirring occasionally, until tender and golden brown, about 20 minutes.

NUTRITIONAL INFORMATION
Per Serving

Calories:	90
Total Fat:	3.8 g
Cholesterol:	2.5 mg
Sodium:	191 mg
Total Carbohydrates:	13.6 g
Fiber:	9 g
Sugars:	1 g
Protein:	3 g

Prep time:	5 min.
Cook time:	20 min.
Total time:	25 min.
Yield:	4 servings
Serving size:	3/4 c.

Exotic Mushroom Ragout

INGREDIENTS

1/2 lb. assorted mushrooms
    (shiitake, oyster, cremini), chopped

1 1/2 tbsp. extra-virgin olive oil

1/4 tsp. kosher salt

1/4 tsp. ground black pepper

1/2 c. marinara sauce

DIRECTIONS

Heat oil in a 12-inch nonstick skillet over medium-high heat. Add mushrooms, and season with salt and pepper. Sauté mushrooms until tender and liquid has evaporated, about 10 minutes.

Stir in marinara sauce, bring to a simmer, and cook for an additional 10 minutes.

NUTRITIONAL INFORMATION
Per Serving

Calories:	99
Total Fat:	6.5 g
Cholesterol:	3.7 mg
Sodium:	283 mg
Total Carbohydrates:	7.5 g
Fiber:	1.6 g
Sugars:	0 g
Protein:	0 g

Prep time:	10 min.
Cook time:	20 min.
Total time:	30 min.
Yield:	4 servings
Serving size:	3/4 c.

Roasted Cauliflower

INGREDIENTS

1 medium head cauliflower, cut into florets

2 tbsp. extra-virgin olive oil

1/4 tsp. kosher salt

1/4 tsp. ground black pepper

DIRECTIONS

Preheat oven to 450 degrees. Place cauliflower florets on a rimmed baking sheet, and toss with oil, salt and pepper. Spread florets out, and roast stirring occasionally, until tender and golden brown, about 20 minutes.

NUTRITIONAL INFORMATION
Per Serving

Calories:	96
Total Fat:	7 g
Cholesterol:	50 mg
Sodium:	187 mg
Total Carbohydrates:	5.5 g
Fiber:	2.6 g
Sugars:	2.6 g
Protein:	3.6 g

Prep time:	5 min.
Cook time:	20 min.
Total time:	25 min.
Yield:	4 servings
Serving size:	1 c.

Oven Roasted Bell Peppers

INGREDIENTS

3 bell peppers (green, red, orange, and/or yellow)

2 tbsp. extra-virgin olive oil

1/4 tsp. kosher salt

1/4 tsp. ground black pepper

DIRECTIONS

Preheat oven to 350 degrees. Place pepper halves on a rimmed baking sheet, and toss with oil, salt and pepper. Spread peppers out cut-side down, and roast until the peppers begin to brown, about 25 minutes. Transfer peppers to a large bowl and cover with plastic wrap until they're cool enough to handle. Once cool, peel skin off peppers and slice into 1/2-inch strips.

NUTRITIONAL INFORMATION
Per Serving

Calories:	87
Total Fat:	7 g
Cholesterol:	5 mg
Sodium:	126 mg
Total Carbohydrates:	5 g
Fiber:	1.9 g
Sugars:	3 g
Protein:	0.8 g

Prep time:	5 min.
Cook time:	25 min.
Total time:	30 min.
Yield:	4 servings
Serving size:	1/2 c.

Grilled Italian Eggplant

INGREDIENTS

1 lb. Italian eggplant,
  cut into 3/4" thick rounds

3 tbsp. extra-virgin olive oil

1/4 tsp. kosher salt

1/4 tsp. ground black pepper

DIRECTIONS

Preheat grill according to manufacturer's directions or set grill pan over medium-high heat. Brush eggplant slices with oil on both sides, and season with salt and pepper. Brush grill rack with oil, and grill eggplant until browned, turning occasionally, 12-15 minutes.

NUTRITIONAL INFORMATION
Per Serving

Calories:	80
Total Fat:	3.8 g
Cholesterol:	2.5 mg
Sodium:	275 mg
Total Carbohydrates:	10 g
Fiber:	4.5 g
Sugars:	2.5 g
Protein:	4 g

Prep time:	10 min.
Cook time:	15 min.
Total time:	25 min.
Yield:	4 servings
Serving size:	1/4 grilled eggplant

Oven Roasted Plum Tomatoes

INGREDIENTS

4 plum tomatoes, halved
  and seeds removed

1 tbsp. extra-virgin olive oil

1/4 tsp. kosher salt

1/4 tsp. ground black pepper

1 tbsp. minced parsley

DIRECTIONS

Preheat oven to 400 degrees. Place tomato halves on a rimmed baking sheet, and toss with oil, salt and pepper. Spread tomatoes out cut-side up, and roast until the tomatoes begin to caramelize, about 20 minutes. Finish tomatoes with parsley, and serve.

NUTRITIONAL INFORMATION
Per Serving

Calories:	52
Total Fat:	3.7 g
Cholesterol:	2.5 mg
Sodium:	129 mg
Total Carbohydrates:	5 g
Fiber:	1.5 g
Sugars:	3.2 g
Protein:	1 g

Prep time:	5 min.
Cook time:	20 min.
Total time:	25 min.
Yield:	4 servings
Serving size:	2 tomato halves

Black Barley

INGREDIENTS

1/2 c. black barley, rinsed

1 tsp. kosher salt

1/4 tsp. ground black pepper

DIRECTIONS

Bring 3 cups water to a boil in a heavy saucepan. Add barley and salt, cover tightly, and return to a boil. Reduce heat and simmer until barley is tender, 35-40 minutes. Drain excess liquid if necessary, transfer to a bowl, and season with black pepper before serving.

NUTRITIONAL INFORMATION
Per Serving

Calories:	120
Total Fat:	1 g
Cholesterol:	0 mg
Sodium:	253 mg
Total Carbohydrates:	24 g
Fiber:	5 g
Sugars:	0 g
Protein:	4 g

Prep time:	5 min.
Cook time:	40 min.
Total time:	45 min.
Yield:	4 servings
Serving size:	1/2 c.

Sun-Dried Tomato Couscous

INGREDIENTS

1 1/2 c. low-sodium chicken broth

1 1/2 c. couscous

1/2 c. oil packed sun-dried tomatoes, drained and diced

1/4 tsp. kosher salt

1/4 tsp. ground black pepper

DIRECTIONS

Bring broth to a boil in a saucepan over medium heat. Stir in couscous and sun-dried tomatoes, take off heat and cover. Let sit 10 minutes, season with salt and pepper, fluff with a fork, and serve.

NUTRITIONAL INFORMATION
Per Serving

Calories:	237
Total Fat:	2 g
Cholesterol:	0 mg
Sodium:	186 mg
Total Carbohydrates:	45 g
Fiber:	3 g
Sugars:	1 g
Protein:	8 g

Prep time:	5 min.
Cook time:	15 min.
Total time:	20 min.
Yield:	4 servings
Serving size:	3/4 c.

Red Bell Pepper Orzo

INGREDIENTS

2 qt. water

1 c. orzo

3/4 c. diced roasted red bell pepper

1/4 tsp. kosher salt

1/4 tsp. ground black pepper

DIRECTIONS

Bring water to a boil in a saucepan over medium-high heat. Stir in orzo and cook uncovered until al dente, about 10 minutes. Drain and transfer to a serving bowl, and toss with remaining ingredients.

NUTRITIONAL INFORMATION
Per Serving

Calories:	168
Total Fat:	0 g
Cholesterol:	0 mg
Sodium:	260 mg
Total Carbohydrates:	33 g
Fiber:	1.7 g
Sugars:	2.6 g
Protein:	6 g

Prep time:	5 min.
Cook time:	15 min.
Total time:	20 min.
Yield:	4 servings
Serving size:	1/2 c.

Roasted Water Chestnuts

INGREDIENTS

2   8 oz. cans water chestnuts, drained and rinsed

2 tbsp. extra-virgin olive oil

1/4 tsp. kosher salt

1/4 tsp. ground black pepper

DIRECTIONS

Preheat oven to 400 degrees. Place water chestnuts on a rimmed baking sheet, and toss with oil, salt and pepper. Spread them out and roast stirring once, until golden brown, 10-15 minutes.

NUTRITIONAL INFORMATION
Per Serving

Calories:	84
Total Fat:	7 g
Cholesterol:	5 mg
Sodium:	132 mg
Total Carbohydrates:	5 g
Fiber:	1 g
Sugars:	2g
Protein:	1g

Prep time:	5 min
Cook time:	15 min
Total time:	20 min
Yield:	4 servings
Serving size:	1/2 c.

Sautéed Spinach

INGREDIENTS

1 lb. baby spinach
1 tbsp. extra-virgin olive oil
1/4 tsp. kosher salt
1/4 tsp. ground black pepper

DIRECTIONS

Heat oil in a 12-inch nonstick skillet over medium-high heat. Add spinach and cook, stirring until spinach is wilted, about 5 minutes. Remove pan from heat, season with salt and pepper, and serve.

NUTRITIONAL INFORMATION
Per Serving

Calories:	57
Total Fat:	3.5 g
Cholesterol:	2.5 mg
Sodium:	209 mg
Total Carbohydrates:	4 g
Fiber:	2.7 g
Sugars:	0 g
Protein:	2.6 g

Prep time:	5 min.
Cook time:	5 min.
Total time:	10 min.
Yield:	4 servings
Serving size:	1/2 c.

Spaghetti Squash with Fresh Basil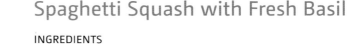

INGREDIENTS

1 3 to 3 1/2 lb. spaghetti squash
1/4 c. chopped basil
1/4 tsp. kosher salt
1/4 tsp. ground black pepper

DIRECTIONS

Pierce squash with a small sharp knife. Place squash in a microwave-safe bowl, and cook in the microwave 8 minutes. Turn squash over and continue to cook until squash gives when pressed gently, 8 -10 minutes more. Remove squash from microwave and allow to cool 5 minutes. Carefully cut squash in half, remove seeds and scrape out squash flesh into a large b[...] Toss with remaining ingredi[...] and serve.

NUTRITIONAL INFORMATION
Per Serving

Calories:	9[...]
Total Fat:	1 g
Cholesterol:	0 mg
Sodium:	184 mg
Total Carbohydrates:	22 g
Fiber:	5 g
Sugars:	8 g
Protein:	2 g

Prep time:	5 min.
Cook time:	20 min.
Total time:	25 min.
Yield:	4 servings
Serving size:	1/2 c.

Curried Cauliflower Mash

INGREDIENTS

1 medium head cauliflower, cut
 into florets

1/4 tsp. kosher salt

1/2 tsp. ground black pepper

1 tbsp. Thai red curry paste

DIRECTIONS

In a large pot of boiling salted water,
add cauliflower florets and cook until
tender, 6-10 minutes. Drain cauliflower and place in a food processor,
add pepper and curry paste, and
puree until smooth.

NUTRITIONAL INFORMATION
Per Serving

Calories:	34
Total Fat:	1 g
Cholesterol:	0 mg
Sodium:	395 mg
Total Carbohydrates:	5 g
Fiber:	2 g
Sugars:	3 g
Protein:	2 g

Prep time:	5 min.
Cook time:	15 min.
Total time:	20 min.
Yield:	4 servings
Serving size:	1/2 c.

Maple Glazed Turnips

INGREDIENTS

1 lb. small turnips, peeled and cut
 into 1/2" wedges

1 tbsp. extra-virgin olive oil

2 tbsp. maple syrup

1/4 tsp. kosher salt

1/4 tsp. ground black pepper

DIRECTIONS

Preheat oven to 400 degrees. Place
turnips on a rimmed baking sheet,
and toss with oil, maple syrup, salt
and pepper. Spread turnips out and
roast stirring once, until tender and
golden brown, 20-30 minutes.

NUTRITIONAL INFORMATION
Per Serving

Calories:	87
Total Fat:	3.6 g
Cholesterol:	2.5 mg
Sodium:	200 mg
Total Carbohydrates:	14 g
Fiber:	2 g
Sugars:	10 g
Protein:	1 g

Prep time:	5 min.
Cook time:	30 min.
Total time:	35 min.
Yield:	4 servings
Serving size:	1/2 c.

Carrot & Rutabaga Mash

INGREDIENTS

1 medium sized rutabaga, peeled and diced

2 carrots, peeled and chopped

1/2 tsp. kosher salt

1/2 tsp. ground black pepper

DIRECTIONS

Place rutabaga and carrots in a large heavy bottom saucepan with water to cover over medium heat. Bring to a boil, add salt and cook until vegetables are tender, 30-40 minutes. Drain and place in a food processor, season with pepper, and puree until smooth.

NUTRITIONAL INFORMATION
Per Serving

Calories:	3
Total Fat:	0
Cholesterol:	0 m
Sodium:	270 m
Total Carbohydrates:	7
Fiber:	2
Sugars:	4
Protein:	1

Prep time:	10 min.
Cook time:	40 min.
Total time:	50 min.
Yield:	4 servings
Serving size:	1/2 c.

Herbed Parsnip Mash

INGREDIENTS

1 1/2 lbs. parsnips, peeled and sliced

1 tsp. kosher salt

1 tbsp. chopped basil

1 tbsp. chopped parsley

1/2 tbsp. chopped oregano

1/4 tsp. ground black pepper

DIRECTIONS

In a large pot cover parsnips with water and bring to a boil over medium-high heat. Add salt, reduce heat and cook until tender, 15-20 minutes. Drain parsnips and place in a food processor, add remaining ingredients, and puree until smooth.

NUTRITIONAL INFORMATION
Per Serving

Calories:	102
Total Fat:	0 g
Cholesterol:	0 mg
Sodium:	260 mg
Total Carbohydrates:	24 g
Fiber:	5 g
Sugars:	7 g
Protein:	2 g

Prep time:	5 min.
Cook time:	20 min.
Total time:	25 min.
Yield:	4 servings
Serving size:	1/2 c.

Yellow Squash Tarragon Puree

INGREDIENTS

1 lb. yellow squash, sliced into 1/2" rounds

2 tbsp. chopped fresh tarragon

1/4 tsp. kosher salt

1/4 tsp. ground black pepper

DIRECTIONS

In a steamer set over boiling water, steam squash, covered, until tender, about 5 minutes. Place squash in a food processor, add tarragon, salt and pepper, and puree until smooth.

NUTRITIONAL INFORMATION
Per Serving

Calories:	24
Total Fat:	0 g
Cholesterol:	0 mg
Sodium:	124 mg
Total Carbohydrates:	5 g
Fiber:	1.6 g
Sugars:	3 g
Protein:	1 g

Prep time:	5 min.
Cook time:	10 min.
Total time:	15 min.
Yield:	4 servings
Serving size:	1/2 c.

Sweet Potato & Leek Puree

INGREDIENTS

1 tbsp. extra-virgin olive oil

2 leeks, trimmed and diced

2 large sweet potatoes, peeled and diced

4 c. water

1/4 tsp. kosher salt

1/4 tsp. ground black pepper

DIRECTIONS

Heat oil in a large saucepan over medium heat. Add leeks and cook until soft and translucent. Add sweet potatoes and water, and bring to a boil. Cook until potatoes are tender, about 20 minutes. Drain potatoes and leeks, and place in a food processor, season with salt and pepper, and puree until smooth.

NUTRITIONAL INFORMATION
Per Serving

Calories:	107
Total Fat:	3.7 g
Cholesterol:	2.5 mg
Sodium:	149 mg
Total Carbohydrates:	18 g
Fiber:	2.5 g
Sugars:	5 g
Protein:	1.5 g

Prep time:	10 min.
Cook time:	20 min.
Total time:	30 min.
Yield:	4 servings
Serving size:	1/2 c.

SAVORY SNACKS

NIBBLES, NOSHES AND SAVORY SNACKS TO TICKLE THE PALATE

Endive Cups with Blue Cheese &
Roasted Cumin Walnuts

NUTRITIONAL INFORMATION
Per Serving

Calories:	38
Total Fat:	6 g
Cholesterol:	8 mg
Sodium:	101 mg
Total Carbohydrates:	2 g
Fiber:	1 g
Sugars:	0 g
Protein:	3 g

The leaves of Belgian endive were made for parties; they're firm enough to support the weight of filling, and they're small enough to fit on a cocktail napkin.

INGREDIENTS

1/3 c. chopped walnuts
1/4 tsp. ground cumin
1/3 c. crumbled blue cheese
1/4 c. reduced-fat cream cheese
16 fresh Belgian endive leaves

DIRECTIONS

Adjust oven rack to upper-middle position and heat oven to 400 degrees. Line rimmed baking sheet with parchment. Place walnuts on baking sheet, dust with ground cumin, and roast for 5-6 minutes until nuts are fragrant. Remove from oven to cool.

In food processor, blend blue cheese and cream cheese until creamy. Place cheese mixture in zip-top bag, seal, then cut off 1/4-inch from corner of bag.

Arrange endive leaves on serving plate. Gently squeeze 1 teaspoon of cheese mixture into each endive cup, then sprinkle roasted walnuts on top.

Prep time:	9 min.
Cook time:	0 min.
Total time:	9 min.
Yield:	8 servings
Serving size:	2 endive cups

TOTAL TIME 9 min.

TOTAL TIME 15 min.

Cucumber Cups Filled with Herbed Cheese Topped with Capers

When they talk about a gorgeous medley of flavors, what they really mean to say is The Fresh Diet's Herbed Cheese Cucumber Cups. This appetizer combines the decadence of creamy cheese with the fresh flavors of parsley, basil, oregano and capers. When chopping the fresh herbs, chop the leaves very fine. That way more of the oils and flavors are released. The flavors are fresh and delicious, and they add a dash of color, too. Perfect to serve at a luncheon, dinner party or anywhere you want to impress.

INGREDIENTS

8 1/2" thick cucumber slices

1/2 c. reduced-fat cream cheese, softened

1 tsp. minced parsley

1 tsp. minced basil

1 tsp. minced oregano

1 tbsp. capers

DIRECTIONS

Scoop out cucumber seeds with a melon baller or spoon to create an indentation, leaving the bottom intact. Place on a serving dish, and set aside.

Combine cream cheese, sour cream and herbs in a food processor and process until smooth and creamy. This should take about 1 minute. Place cream cheese mixture in a zip-top bag, seal it, and cut 1/4-inch from bottom corner of bag.

Squeeze 1/8 of the cream cheese mixture into each cucumber. Garnish with capers and serve.

Prep time:	15 min.
Cook time:	0 min.
Total time:	15 min.
Yield:	4 servings
Serving size:	2 cucumber cups

NUTRITIONAL INFORMATION
Per Serving

Calories:	77
Total Fat:	6 g
Cholesterol:	20 mg
Sodium:	184 mg
Total Carbohydrates:	2 g
Fiber:	0 g
Sugars:	1 g
Protein:	2 g

Artichoke Bottoms Filled with Creamy Cauliflower

Cauliflower is a revelation to a lot of dieters. Lightly steam it, puree it, and you'll no longer miss those verboten mashed potatoes.

INGREDIENTS

1/2 c. cauliflower florets cut in 2" pieces
1/4 c. reduced-fat cream cheese
1/8 tsp. salt
Dash ground black pepper
6 canned artichoke bottoms

DIRECTIONS

Bring small saucepan of water to boil over high heat. Cook cauliflower for 7-10 minutes or until tender. Drain and refrigerate until chilled, approximately 30 minutes.

In food processor, combine cauliflower, cream cheese, salt and pepper, and process until smooth and creamy, about 1 minute. Place cauliflower mixture in a zip-top bag, seal it, then cut 1/4-inch from corner of bag.

Place artichoke bottoms on serving dish and squeeze 1/6 of the cauliflower mixture into each artichoke.

Prep time:	5 min.
Cook time:	10 min.
Total time:	15 min.
Yield:	6 servings
Serving Size:	1 artichoke bottom

TOTAL TIME 15 min.

TOTAL TIME 12 min.

Cucumber & Green Papaya Slaw with Low-Fat Yogurt

Give this recipe a try next time you're asked to bring coleslaw to a gathering. This decidedly un-ho-hum coleslaw features unripened papaya often found in spicy Thai cuisine.

INGREDIENTS

1 small green papaya, peeled and seeded
1 English cucumber
1/3 c. reduced-fat plain yogurt
1/4 c. reduced-fat sour cream
1/4 tsp. salt
Dash ground black pepper

DIRECTIONS

Cut papaya into 1/8-inch wide slices, then cut into matchstick-sized pieces. Place in medium-size mixing bowl.

Cut cucumber in half and then lengthwise. Dispose seeds in center, then cut lengths into matchstick-sized pieces and add to papaya. Add yogurt, sour cream, salt and pepper to taste. Mix well and serve.

Prep time:	12 min.
Cook time:	0 min.
Total time:	12 min.
Yield:	6 servings
Serves:	1/4 c. slaw

NUTRITIONAL INFORMATION
Per Serving

Calories:	56
Total Fat:	2 g
Cholesterol:	4 mg
Sodium:	118 mg
Total Carbohydrates:	9 g
Fiber:	1 g
Sugars:	6 g
Protein:	2 g

Grilled Canadian Bacon over Baby Arugula with Fresh Honeydew & Toasted Pine Nuts

NUTRITIONAL INFORMATION
Per Serving

Calories:	98
Total Fat:	6 g
Cholesterol:	12 mg
Sodium:	345 mg
Total Carbohydrates:	7 g
Fiber:	1 g
Sugars:	5 g
Protein:	6 g

Bacon with melon is a classic flavor pairing, and the arugula and pine nuts lend this appetizer a Mediterranean flair. Canadian bacon is juicy instead of crispy, and offers less fat than regular bacon, which puts it within reach for the occasional treat.

Meanwhile, peppery arugula is loaded with iron and vitamins A and C.

INGREDIENTS

6 1/4" wide slices Canadian bacon

12 1/4" wide slices honeydew
  melon, peeled

1/4 c. pine nuts

1 1/2 c. arugula

DIRECTIONS

Set 10-inch skillet over medium-high heat. Place Canadian bacon in pan and cook 4 minutes per side. Remove bacon from pan to cool, then cut each piece of bacon in half.

When skillet is cool enough to touch, carefully wipe away grease with paper towel. Set skillet over medium-high heat and add pine nuts to pan, stirring frequently to prevent burning. Remove nuts from pan when golden and fragrant, approximately 5-7 minutes, and cool.

Divide arugula among six serving plates. Arrange two pieces of bacon and two slices of melon on each salad. Sprinkle with toasted pine nuts.

Prep time:	5 min.
Cook time:	15 min.
Total time:	20 min.
Yield:	6 servings
Serving size:	1 salad

TOTAL TIME 20 min.

TOTAL TIME 15 min.

Black Bean & Avocado Wheat Crostini

Finding an appetizer that will whet your appetite but still leave you wanting more is no easy feat. This spectacular little number does just that. The wheat crostini will satiate a gnawing hunger while the fresh, herby avocado and black bean mix adds an extra zing to keep those tastebuds happy. Black beans contain a high quantity of protein, and the overwhelming health benefits of the "super fruit" avocado make this appetizer a must try.

NUTRITIONAL INFORMATION
Per Serving

Calories:	98
Total Fat:	1.6 g
Cholesterol:	0 mg
Sodium:	244 mg
Total Carbohydrates:	17 g
Fiber:	3 g
Sugars:	0.5 g
Protein:	4 g

INGREDIENTS

8 1/4" thick slices whole wheat
   baguette

1/3 c. diced avocado

1/4 c. diced tomato

1 tbsp. minced red onion

2 tsp. minced jalapeno

1 tsp. minced garlic

1 tbsp. chopped cilantro

1/8 tsp. salt

1/4 tsp. lemon juice

1/2 c. canned black beans,
   drained and rinsed

DIRECTIONS

Preheat the oven to 400 degrees. Place the baguette slices on a baking sheet and toast them in the oven for about 5 minutes or until just crisp. Remove from oven and set the crostini aside.

Place avocado in a small bowl, and mash with a fork. Stir in the remaining ingredients, and refrigerate until ready to use. To assemble, divide the avocado mixture among the crostini, and serve.

Prep time:	10 min.
Cook time:	5 min.
Total time:	15 min.
Yield:	4 servings
Serving size:	2 crostini

Mini Whole Wheat Pockets Filled with Tuna Salad

NUTRITIONAL INFORMATION
Per Serving

Calories:	63
Total Fat:	1.5 g
Cholesterol:	9 mg
Sodium:	299 mg
Total Carbohydrates:	6 g
Fiber:	0 g
Sugars:	0 g
Protein:	6 g

Tuna is a classic. And classics achieve their status for a reason. For healthy eating, canned tuna wins it all. It's rich in protein, low in fat and calories and is an excellent source of the essential omega-3 fatty acids, which help lower blood pressure and cholesterol. These characteristics make it a healthy cook's best friend. Our mini tuna salad pockets are ideal for a working mom's snack on the go, a child's midday nosh or a healthy alternative to tide you over until dinner. It doesn't discriminate, and it appeals to most palates. That's why we love this recipe!

INGREDIENTS

1/2 c. canned albacore tuna, drained

1 1/2 tbsp. reduced fat mayonnaise

2 tsp. low-fat sour cream

1/4 tsp. kosher salt

1/8 tsp. ground black pepper

2 tsp. minced parsley

4 mini whole wheat pita pockets, halved

DIRECTIONS

In a small bowl, mix together tuna, mayonnaise, sour cream, salt, pepper and parsley until well combined. Divide tuna salad among the pocket halves, and serve.

Prep time:	10 min.
Cook time:	0 min.
Total time:	10 min.
Yield:	4 servings
Serving size:	2 mini pita halves

TOTAL TIME **10** min.

TOTAL TIME 16 min.

Balsamic Grilled Eggplant
with Fresh Mozzarella & Basil

If eggplant hasn't won you over yet, try this recipe. The grill gives it a rich meaty flavor, emphasized by the salty cheese and fragrant basil. This dish is best served in the late summer when eggplant and basil are at their finest.

INGREDIENTS

6 1/4" wide round slices of eggplant
2 fresh mozzarella balls, 2 oz. each
2 tbsp. extra virgin olive oil
2 tbsp. balsamic vinegar
6 fresh basil leaves
1/4 tsp. salt
1/8 tsp. ground black pepper

DIRECTIONS

Drizzle balsamic vinegar over eggplant slices and let marinate at room temperature for 10 minutes.

Preheat grill according to manufacturer's directions or set grill pan over medium-high heat.

Using pastry or silicone basting brush, brush eggplant with olive oil before placing on grill. Cook for approximately 3 minutes, then turn eggplant to cook on other side. Remove eggplant from grill and cool for 5 minutes before proceeding with recipe.

Slice mozzarella balls into six slices, then top each slice of eggplant with basil leaf and slice of mozzarella.

Prep time:	10 min.
Cook time:	6 min.
Total time:	16 min.
Yield:	6 servings
Serving size:	1 eggplant round

NUTRITIONAL INFORMATION
Per Serving

Calories:	99
Total Fat:	8 g
Cholesterol:	15 mg
Sodium:	215 mg
Total Carbohydrates:	3 g
Fiber:	2 g
Sugars:	1 g
Protein:	5 g

Mushroom Crowns Filled with Pesto Chicken

NUTRITIONAL INFORMATION
Per Serving

Calories:	59
Total Fat:	6 g
Cholesterol:	4 mg
Sodium:	23 mg
Total Carbohydrates:	1 g
Fiber:	1 g
Sugars:	0 g
Protein:	2 g

This mouth-watering appetizer will become a dinner party favorite once your guests taste the savory blend of mushrooms and chicken. Watch the crowns vanish from that serving platter!

INGREDIENTS

20 cremini mushroom crowns
1/4 c. chopped fresh basil
2 tbsp. chopped fresh parsley
2 tbsp. pine nuts
2 tbsp. shredded Parmesan cheese
3 tbsp. extra virgin olive oil
1/4 tsp. salt
1/8 tsp. ground black pepper
12 oz. ground chicken breast

DIRECTIONS

Adjust oven rack to upper-middle position and heat oven to 350 degrees. Line rimmed baking sheet with foil and place mushroom crowns gill-side up on foil.

In food processor, combine all ingredients except ground chicken, then process until smooth. In medium mixing bowl, combine pesto sauce with ground chicken, using your hands to mix sauce with meat.

Place heaping tablespoon-sized portions of chicken mixture onto each mushroom crown. Bake for 15 -20 minutes until chicken mixture is completely cooked through and mushrooms are softened.

Prep time:	10 min.
Cook time:	20 min.
Total time:	30 min.
Yield:	10 servings
Serving size:	2 stuffed mushrooms

TOTAL TIME 30 min.

TOTAL TIME **13** min.

Teriyaki Salmon & Caper Salad
with Whole Wheat Crostini

Capers, the tiny buds of a bush native to the Mediterranean, make a piquant addition to this salad filled with bold flavors.

INGREDIENTS

8 oz. fresh salmon filet, skin removed and cut into 1" pieces (8 1 oz. cubes)

1/4 c. reduced-sodium soy sauce

2 tbsp. honey

16 1/4" thick slices whole wheat baguette

1 c. spring mix lettuce

1 tbsp. bottled capers, drained

Cooking spray

DIRECTIONS

Place salmon pieces in small mixing bowl. Stir soy sauce and honey together in liquid measuring cup, and pour over salmon. Cover mixing bowl with plastic wrap and marinate in refrigerator for 45 minutes.

Meanwhile, preheat the oven to 400 degrees. Place the baguette slices on a baking sheet and toast them in the oven for about 5 minutes or until just crisp. Remove from oven and set aside.

Place small skillet over medium-high heat. Spray pan with cooking spray and cook salmon until golden brown outside, turning frequently to cook pieces evenly, approximately 1-2 minutes. Set salmon aside to cool for 15 minutes. When ready to serve, divide lettuce among four salad plates, then top each with two pieces of salmon. Garnish with capers.

Prep time: 5 min.
Cook time: 8 min.
Total time: 13 min.
Yield: 8 servings
Serving Size: 1 salad
                 & 2 crostini

NUTRITIONAL INFORMATION
Per Serving

Calories:	123
Total Fat:	3 g
Cholesterol:	14 mg
Sodium:	515 mg
Total Carbohydrates:	16 g
Fiber:	1 g
Sugars:	4 g
Protein:	9 g

Mini Whole Wheat Sweet & Sour Sloppy Joes

NUTRITIONAL INFORMATION
Per Serving

Calories:	122
Total Fat:	3 g
Cholesterol:	35 mg
Sodium:	336 mg
Total Carbohydrates:	9 g
Fiber:	1 g
Sugars:	4 g
Protein:	13 g

Sloppy Joes seem to remind everyone of childhood; these mini versions will bring a smile to your face, deliver some zippy flavor to your taste buds – and spare you some extra calories.

INGREDIENTS

1 lb. 95% lean ground beef
3/4 c. sweet and sour sauce
1/4 c. water
1/2 tsp. salt
1/8 tsp. ground black pepper
1 12" whole wheat baguette

DIRECTIONS

Set 10-inch skillet over medium-high heat. Add ground beef, salt and pepper, then break up ground beef with spatula in pan. Cook until beef is browned and cooked through. Remove excess fat by carefully tilting pan to side and spooning away liquid fat collecting on bottom.

Reduce heat to medium low and add sweet and sour sauce and water. Cook for 10 more minutes, stirring occasionally to prevent meat from sticking to pan.

While sauce cooks, cut baguette into eight pieces (approximately 1 1/2-inch wide), then cut each piece through middle, sandwich-style. Place 1/8 of meat on bottom of each baguette piece, top with other half, and serve.

Prep time:	5 min.
Cook time:	15 min.
Total time:	20 min.
Yield:	8 servings
Serving Size:	1 Sloppy Joe

TOTAL TIME 11 min.

Grilled Mahi Mahi & Cherry Tomato Skewer

This appetizer bursts with health and flavor. In those moments when you need something to fill the gap, but understand your body's requirements for the freshest vegetables and proteins, this is the hero to call. Mahi mahi is a great fish for grilling. It has a nice meaty texture and great flavor. And the best part: It's just as fun to make on skewers as it is to eat them!

INGREDIENTS

6 oz. Mahi mahi, cut into
   1/2" cubes
8 cherry tomatoes
4 wooden skewers, soaked in water
   for 20 minutes

DIRECTIONS

Preheat grill according to manufacturer's directions or set grill pan over medium-high heat. Thread two pieces of mahi mahi and two tomatoes on each skewer. Grill skewers 2-3 minutes per side.

Prep time:	5 min.
Cook time:	6 min.
Total time:	11 min.
Yield:	4 servings
Serving size:	1 skewer

NUTRITIONAL INFORMATION
Per Serving

Calories:	44
Total Fat:	0 g
Cholesterol:	33 mg
Sodium:	41 mg
Total Carbohydrates:	1 g
Fiber:	0 g
Sugars:	0 g
Protein:	8 g

Grilled Shrimp Skewer with Fresh Mango Salsa

NUTRITIONAL INFORMATION
Per Serving

Calories:	20
Total Fat:	0 g
Cholesterol:	13 mg
Sodium:	182 mg
Total Carbohydrates:	3 g
Fiber:	0 g
Sugars:	2.8 g
Protein:	1.6 g

This dish is for the more adventurous palate. The sweetness of the mango is perfectly complemented by the sharpness of the red onion. Shrimp are a great base to work with as they soak up the flavors they are cooked with beautifully. Luckily the flavors we use are not high in fat and polyunsaturated oils like most shrimp sauces. This is one of those appetizers that will leave you smacking your lips and reminding yourself to make it again.

When buying shrimp, the main advantage to using the count is that it's a reliable, consistent measure. Adjectives that describe the size, like "jumbo" or "large," aren't used consistently. The 16/20 count shrimp are large enough to thread the skewer through two spots, holding them more securely on.

INGREDIENTS

1/2 c. diced mango

1 tbsp. red onion

1 tsp. apple cider vinegar

1 tbsp. cilantro

6 16/20 count shrimp, tail-on, peeled and deveined

1/4 tsp. kosher salt

1/4 tsp. ground black pepper

4 4" wooden skewers, soaked in water for 20 minutes

DIRECTIONS

Preheat grill according to manufacturer's directions or set grill pan over medium-high heat.

In a small bowl, combine mango, onion, vinegar and cilantro. Refrigerate until ready to use.

Thread two pieces of shrimp on each skewer, and season with salt and pepper. Grill shrimp 2-3 minutes per side. Serve with mango salsa.

Prep time:	5 min.
Cook time:	6 min.
Total time:	11 min.
Yield:	4 servings
Serving size:	1 skewer

TOTAL TIME **11** min.

TOTAL TIME 12 min.

Mandarin Duck Pancakes with Scallions

If you miss the all-you-can-eat buffets at Chinese restaurants, here's a recipe that's so easy to make at home. Look for smoked duck breast in specialty meat departments.

Don't want to heat up the grill? Substitute raw scallions for the grilled.

INGREDIENTS

- 4 oz. smoked duck breast, chilled, and cut into 6 evenly sized strips
- 2 tbsp. bottled duck sauce
- 2 scallions, white end trimmed off
- 4 whole wheat tortillas, 5" diameter

DIRECTIONS

Preheat grill according to manufacturer's directions or set grill pan over medium-high heat. Grill scallions until limp and just beginning to brown, then remove from grill and cut in half.

Place tortillas on flat surface and spread 1 1/2 teaspoon of duck sauce on each tortilla. Then top with piece of duck breast and half scallion. Roll tortilla from bottom to top. Cut in half before serving.

Prep time:	10 min.
Cook time:	2 min.
Total time:	12 min.
Yield:	4 servings
Serving size:	1 pancake

NUTRITIONAL INFORMATION
Per Serving

Calories:	116
Total Fat:	2 g
Cholesterol:	22 mg
Sodium:	204 mg
Total Carbohydrates:	18 g
Fiber:	4 g
Sugars:	5 g
Protein:	9 g

Mini Sweet Potato & Turkey Shepherd's Pie

NUTRITIONAL INFORMATION
Per Serving

Calories:	134
Total Fat:	5 g
Cholesterol:	62 mg
Sodium:	234 mg
Total Carbohydrates:	10 g
Fiber:	1 g
Sugars:	2 g
Protein:	13 g

In some circles, shepherd's pie is favorite fare with its succulent nuggets of meat, choice veggies and oven-crisp topping of whipped potatoes. British cooks developed the dish as a way to use up leftovers from their Sunday roast. We've given this classic recipe a fresh spin, substituting turkey for beef, spicing it with Chinese five-spice powder, and topping it all off with sweet spuds.

INGREDIENTS

1 lbs. ground turkey
1/4 c. corn flake crumbs
1 large egg
1/2 tsp. salt
1/8 tsp. ground black pepper
1/8 tsp. Chinese five-spice powder
2 sweet potatoes, peeled and cut
 into quarters
1/4 c. frozen baby peas, thawed
 cooking spray

DIRECTIONS

Adjust oven rack to upper-middle position and heat oven to 300 degrees. Spray 8" x 8" Pyrex baking dish with cooking spray and set aside.

In bowl of standing mixer, combine ground turkey, egg, salt, pepper, Chinese five-spice powder and corn flake crumbs; then, mix on low until well combined. Alternatively, combine ingredients in large mixing bowl by hand.

Place meat mixture in Pyrex baking dish and spread evenly in 3/4-inch layer. Bake for 20-25 minutes until meat is cooked through.

While meat cooks, fill medium saucepan with water; bring to boil over high heat. Add sweet potatoes, reduce heat to medium high, and cook until fork tender, approximately 15-20 minutes. Remove sweet potatoes from water and place in small mixing bowl. Mash with potato masher until smooth. With spatula, spread mashed sweet potato atop cooked turkey. Garnish with baby peas.

Prep time:	10 min.
Cook time:	25 min.
Total time:	35 min.
Yield:	8 servings
Serving size:	1 square

TOTAL TIME 35 min.

DESSERT

OH, SO SWEET ... OH, SO GOOD!

Mixed Fresh Berries with Creamy Ricotta Cheese Dip

NUTRITIONAL INFORMATION
Per Serving

Calories:	85
Total Fat:	2.7 g
Cholesterol:	9.5 mg
Sodium:	39 mg
Total Carbohydrates:	12 g
Fiber:	2.8 g
Sugars:	7 g
Protein:	4 g

For those of you who like to finish a meal with a sweet burst of freshness, this is the perfect dessert for you! Its light, sweet and deliciously tart. Berries are a power punch in the health department too. They're loaded with fiber, which helps you feel full (and eat less). And they top the charts in antioxidant power, protecting your body against inflammation and free radicals, molecules that can damage cells and organs. If this isn't the answer to many a dieters' wishes, we don't know what is!

INGREDIENTS

1/2 c. part-skim ricotta cheese

1 tbsp. evaporated cane
   juice sugar

1 tsp. lemon zest

1/2 c. blackberries

1/2 c. raspberries

1/2 c. blueberries

1/2 c. strawberries, hulled
   and quartered

DIRECTIONS

Combine ricotta, sugar, and lemon zest in a small bowl and mix well, set aside. In a medium bowl, toss the berries together and divide between four dessert plates, top with lemon ricotta and serve.

Prep time:	10 min.
Cook time:	0 min.
Total time:	10 min.
Yield:	4 servings
Serving size:	1/2 c. mixed berries
	2 tbsp. ricotta cheese

TOTAL TIME **10** min.

TOTAL TIME 12 min.

Sliced Asian Pears with Ricotta Cheese
& Honey Roasted Cashews

In Asia, these pears are often given as gifts because of their high cost. We like the contrast of the pear's delicate flavor with the creamy richness of the ricotta and sweetness of the cashews.

INGREDIENTS

1/4 c. cashew pieces, roasted and unsalted

1 tbsp. honey

1 Asian pear

1/2 c. part-skim ricotta cheese

DIRECTIONS

Adjust oven rack to upper-middle position and heat oven to 375 degrees. Line rimmed baking sheet with parchment or foil and set aside.

In small mixing bowl, stir cashews and honey together until nuts are well coated. Place cashews on baking sheet and bake for 5 minutes, or until nuts are slightly golden and fragrant. Remove from oven, place on small plate, and refrigerate until cool, about an hour.

When ready to serve, slice pear into eight lengthwise pieces and remove seeds. Place two pear slices on each serving dish, and top each portion with 2 tablespoons of ricotta. Divide the roasted cashew pieces among all 4 servings, scattering them across ricotta.

Prep time:	7 min.
Cook time:	5 min.
Total time:	12 min.
Yield:	4 servings
Serving size:	2 pear slices with 2 tbsp. ricotta cheese & 1 tbsp. cashew pieces

NUTRITIONAL INFORMATION
Per Serving

Calories:	117
Total Fat:	6 g
Cholesterol:	10 mg
Sodium:	39 mg
Total Carbohydrates:	11 g
Fiber:	1 g
Sugars:	7 g
Protein:	5 g

Pistachio Crusted Chocolate Dipped Figs

NUTRITIONAL INFORMATION
Per Serving

Calories:	115
Total Fat:	5 g
Cholesterol:	0 mg
Sodium:	3 mg
Total Carbohydrates:	17 g
Fiber:	3 g
Sugars:	13 g
Protein:	2 g

Last-minute dinner guests? Here's a quick dessert you can pull together that's as healthy as it is tasty.

INGREDIENTS

1/4 c. bittersweet chocolate chips

12 dried figs

1/3 c. pistachios, roasted and unsalted

DIRECTIONS

Place sheet of parchment or wax paper on large plate.

Chop pistachios into small pieces with sharp knife or food processor, put on plate, and set aside.

Place chocolate chips in microwave-safe bowl and heat on high for 10 seconds. Stir chocolate and heat for another 10 seconds, repeating until chocolate is completely melted.

Allow to cool for 5 minutes before taking next step.

Dip one fig into melted chocolate and roll in chopped pistachios before setting fig on paper-lined plate; repeat with remaining figs. Refrigerate figs for 20 minutes before serving.

Prep time:	15 min.
Cook time:	1 min.
Total time:	16 min.
Yield:	6 servings
Serving size:	2 figs

TOTAL TIME **16** min.

TOTAL TIME **11** min.

Chocolate Dipped Strawberries
with Creamy Vanilla Ricotta Cheese

Make this recipe when strawberries are at their finest — between late May and early July, depending where you live.

INGREDIENTS

1/3 c. bittersweet chocolate chips

12 medium strawberries, stems attached

1 c. part skim ricotta cheese

1/2 tsp. vanilla extract

DIRECTIONS

Place sheet of parchment or wax paper on large plate, then place strawberries on plate and set aside.

Put chocolate chips in microwave-safe bowl and heat on high for 10 seconds. Stir chocolate and heat for another 10 seconds, repeating process until chocolate is completely melted. Cool for 3-5 minutes.

Dip strawberries into chocolate and place them back on lined plate. Refrigerate for 20 minutes.

While strawberries chill, place ricotta cheese and vanilla extract in small mixing bowl and beat until well combined. Serve with strawberries.

Prep time:	10 min.
Cook time:	1 min.
Total time:	11 min.
Yield:	6 servings
Serving size:	2 strawberries with 2 tbsp. ricotta cheese

NUTRITIONAL INFORMATION
Per Serving

Calories:	111
Total Fat:	6 g
Cholesterol:	13 mg
Sodium:	53 mg
Total Carbohydrates:	10 g
Fiber:	1 g
Sugars:	7 g
Protein:	5 g

Sautéed Pineapple with Key Lime Yogurt Topped with Toasted Coconut Flakes

NUTRITIONAL INFORMATION
Per Serving

Calories:	109
Total Fat:	3 g
Cholesterol:	5 mg
Sodium:	43 mg
Total Carbohydrates:	18 g
Fiber:	1 g
Sugars:	16 g
Protein:	3 g

If fresh pineapple was a taste revelation to you the first time you had it, try it sautéed.

INGREDIENTS

2 c. chopped fresh pineapple, cut into 1/4" wide pieces

1 tbsp. extra virgin olive oil

1 1/2 c. reduced fat plain yogurt

1/4 c. key lime juice (juice from 3 limes)

1/4 c. evaporated cane juice sugar

DIRECTIONS

Set sauté pan over medium-high heat and add oil to pan. When oil begins to shimmer, add pineapple and sauté until golden brown and crispy, approximately 10 minutes. Remove pineapple from pan to large plate and refrigerate until completely cooled, about 2 hours.

When ready to serve, combine yogurt, sugar and key lime juice in small bowl and mix well. Divide yogurt among four small cups, place chilled pineapple slices on top and serve.

Prep time:	5 min.
Cook time:	10 min.
Total time:	15 min.
Yield:	6 servings
Serving size:	1/3 c. pineapple & 1/3 c. yogurt

TOTAL TIME 15 min.

TOTAL TIME 15 min.

Chocolate Pudding Topped with Toasted Almonds

Chocolate pudding and dieting don't often go hand in hand. But we know the right people. Chef Yos has managed to combine the two into a delicately balanced sculpture of delight, decadence and diet. It's the final musical note to end a good meal on. Chocolate comes with its list of health benefits too, but we're inclined to think the sheer joy this pudding brings to any table is enough of a health reason of its own!

INGREDIENTS

2 1/3 c. 1% milk, divided

1 large egg

1/4 c. evaporated cane juice sugar

1/4 c. cocoa powder

2 tbsp. cornstarch

1/8 tsp. sea salt

2 tbsp. bittersweet chocolate chips

2 tsp. vanilla extract

1/4 c. toasted sliced almonds

DIRECTIONS

In a 2 quart heavy saucepan, whisk 1/3 cup milk, egg, sugar, cocoa, cornstarch and salt together until smooth. Slowly whisk in rest of milk and place pan over medium heat. Bring to boil, whisking occasionally and reduce heat. Simmer until thickened, whisking constantly, until thickened, 5-7 minutes. Remove from heat; add chocolate and vanilla, stirring until chocolate has melted. Transfer to a bowl, cover with plastic wrap and refrigerate at least 3 hours or overnight, until set. Garnish with toasted almonds before serving.

Prep time: 5 min.
Cook time: 10 min.
Total time: 15 min.
Yield: 4 servings
Serving size: 1/2 c.

NUTRITIONAL INFORMATION
Per Serving

Calories:	186
Total Fat:	5.7 g
Cholesterol:	53.5 mg
Sodium:	150 mg
Total Carbohydrates:	29 g
Fiber:	2 g
Sugars:	22 g
Protein:	8 g

Ginger Poached Apple with Mascarpone Cheese

Here's a fruit dessert you can enjoy throughout the four seasons, but fall apples will make it even more special.

NUTRITIONAL INFORMATION
Per Serving

Calories:	115
Total Fat:	7 g
Cholesterol:	18 mg
Sodium:	20 mg
Total Carbohydrates:	14 g
Fiber:	2 g
Sugars:	10 g
Protein:	1 g

INGREDIENTS

4 c. water

1 tbsp. ground ginger

2 small apples, peeled and cut in half

4 tbsp. mascarpone cheese

DIRECTIONS

In medium saucepan set over medium-high heat, bring water and ground ginger to boil.

While water is heating, use melon baller or small spoon to remove core and seeds from each apple half. Then, scoop out small well in center to hold cheese. Place apples in boiling water, reduce heat to low, and cook for 20 to 25 minutes until apples are tender, but not mushy. Scoop apples from water, drain, and place on plate to chill for 2 hours in refrigerator.

When ready to serve, remove apples from refrigerator and place mascarpone cheese in small zip-top plastic bag. Snip off 1/8" of one bottom corner of bag with scissors, then squeeze 1 tablespoon of cheese into each apple half.

Prep time:	5 min.
Cook time:	25 min.
Total time:	30 min.
Yield:	4 servings
Serving size:	1 half apple with 1 tbsp. mascarpone cheese

TOTAL TIME **30** min.

TOTAL TIME **40** min.

Maple Baked Pear Filled with Mascarpone Cheese & Crusted with Crunchy Oats

This recipe conjures up images of warm kitchens, crackling fires and lots of laughter. It's a warm, hearty recipe that delights the senses with its flavors and textures. The softness of the baked pear, mingled with the sweetness of the maple and the crunchiness of the oats, work together in perfect harmony. A beautiful celebration of natural ingredients for a healthy indulgence.

To keep the calorie count of this recipe down, look out for granola that is low in saturated fat, higher in polyunsaturated fats and contains less that 10 grams of sugar per serving.

INGREDIENTS

2 ripe but firm Bosc pears, peeled, halved and cored

1 tbsp. maple syrup

4 tbsp. mascarpone cheese

1/4 c. granola

DIRECTIONS

Preheat oven to 400 degrees. Place pears cut side up in an 8-inch glass baking dish and drizzle with maple syrup. Bake until tender and beginning to brown, about 35 minutes. Spoon pears onto dessert plates and drizzle with pan juices. Top with mascarpone cheese and granola and serve.

Prep time: 5 min.
Cook time: 35 min.
Total time: 40 min.
Yield: 4 servings
Serving size: 1 half pear
                with 1 tbsp.
                mascarpone cheese
                & 1 tbsp. granola

NUTRITIONAL INFORMATION
Per Serving

Calories:	218
Total Fat:	15 g
Cholesterol:	35 mg
Sodium:	18 mg
Total Carbohydrates:	20 g
Fiber:	3 g
Sugars:	12.6 g
Protein:	3.4 g

Cherry Maple Oatmeal Cookies

NUTRITIONAL INFORMATION
Per Serving

Calories:	197
Total Fat:	4 g
Cholesterol:	16 mg
Sodium:	142 mg
Total Carbohydrates:	38 g
Fiber:	2 g
Sugars:	24 g
Protein:	3 g

While we think the marriage of cherry and maple in these cookies is sublime, you can substitute with most any dried fruit in this cookie recipe – try them with raisins, currants, dried cranberries or dried blueberries. Look for dried fruit that's free of added sugar and sulfur dioxide, a preservative that's commonly used to prevent the fruit from browning, as some people are sensitive to its presence.

INGREDIENTS

1/4 c. Smart Balance Buttery Spread, softened
1/2 c. light brown sugar, lightly packed in cup
1/2 c. evaporated cane juice sugar
1 large egg
1/2 tsp. vanilla extract
3/4 c. all-purpose flour
1/2 tsp. baking soda
1/2 tsp. ground cinnamon
1/4 tsp. salt
1 1/2 c. quick oats
1/2 c. dried cherries
1/4 c. maple syrup
Cooking spray

DIRECTIONS

Adjust oven rack to upper-middle position and heat oven to 350 degrees. Spray cookie sheet with cooking spray and set aside.
In large mixing bowl or in bowl of standing mixer, beat Smart Balance spread, brown and cane juice sugars until light and creamy. Add egg and vanilla extract, and continue beating until incorporated. Add flour, baking soda, cinnamon and salt and mix until just combined. Stir in oats, dried cherries and maple syrup.

Using tablespoon or small cookie scoop, scoop dough by rounded tablespoonfuls onto cookie sheets. Bake for 8-10 minutes, or until light golden brown. Cool for 10 minutes or longer before serving. Store remaining cookies in airtight container in cool, dry place.

Prep time:	15 min.
Cook time:	20 min.
Total time:	35 min.
Yield:	12 servings
Serving size:	2 cookies

TOTAL TIME 35 min.

TOTAL TIME **43** min.

Lemon Zest Tea Cookies

Fragrant, fresh lemon peel adds lots of zip to recipes, but its sharp flavor can get lost during baking. That's why we substitute a teaspoon of lemon extract to punch up the flavor of these delicious cookies.

INGREDIENTS

1 tsp. lemon extract

1/2 c. 2% milk

1 3/4 c. all-purpose flour

1 tsp. baking powder

1/4 tsp. baking soda

1/4 tsp. salt

1/3 c. Smart Balance Buttery Spread, softened

3/4 c. light brown sugar, lightly packed

1/2 c. sifted confectioners' sugar

1 large egg

1 tsp. grated fresh lemon peel

DIRECTIONS

Adjust oven rack to upper-middle position and heat oven to 350 degrees. Line ungreased cookie sheet with parchment paper and set aside.

Stir lemon extract into milk and set aside. In medium mixing bowl, stir flour, baking powder, baking soda and salt together. In large mixing bowl or bowl of standing mixer, combine Smart Balance spread and sugars, then mix or beat until light and fluffy. Add egg and lemon peel and continue beating until fully combined. Add half of dry ingredients to butter mixture, then add half the milk and mix. Repeat with remaining flour and milk. Mix until dry ingredients are combined.

Drop dough by teaspoonfuls on ungreased cookie sheet and bake for 12-14 minutes, until cookies are golden brown at edges. Repeat with remaining dough. Cool cookies on rack before serving. Store remaining cookies in airtight container in cool, dry place.

Prep time:	15 min.
Cook time:	28 min.
Total time:	43 min.
Yield:	15 servings
Serving size:	2 cookies

NUTRITIONAL INFORMATION
Per Serving

Calories:	145
Total Fat:	4 g
Cholesterol:	13 mg
Sodium:	105 mg
Total Carbohydrates:	26 g
Fiber:	0 g
Sugars:	14 g
Protein:	2 g

Dulce de Leche Sandwich Cookie

NUTRITIONAL INFORMATION
Per Serving

Calories:	176
Total Fat:	4.6 g
Cholesterol:	15 mg
Sodium:	118 mg
Total Carbohydrates:	30 g
Fiber:	0 g
Sugars:	19 g
Protein:	3 g

Another one of our fiercely popular desserts is the one and only Dulce de Leche Sandwich Cookie. Dulce de leche is a thick, creamy caramel like sauce that is the product of slowly simmering down milk and sugar. It is a labor of love, but fear not! You can find this wonderful confection in any Latin market, or in the international food aisle of your local supermarket.

INGREDIENTS

1/2 c. 2% milk

1 3/4 c. unbleached all-purpose flour

1 tsp. baking powder

1/4 tsp. baking soda

1/4 tsp. salt

1/3 c. Smart Balance Buttery Spread, softened

3/4 c. light brown sugar, lightly packed

1/2 c. sifted powdered sugar

1 large egg

1/2 c. dulce de leche

DIRECTIONS

Adjust oven rack to upper-middle position and heat oven to 350 degrees. Line ungreased cookie sheet with parchmxent paper and set aside.

In medium mixing bowl, combine flour, baking powder, baking soda and salt; set aside. In a large mixing bowl, combine Smart Balance spread and sugars and beat until light and fluffy, about 2 minutes.

Add egg and continue beating until fully combined. Reduce speed to low, add flour mixture in two batches, alternating with milk, mix until just combined.

Drop dough by teaspoonfuls on ungreased cookie sheet, spacing about 1 1/2 inches apart and bake until cookies are golden brown at edges, 12-14 minutes. Cool slightly and transfer cookies to a cooling rack to cool completely before filling. Repeat with remaining dough. Spread a teaspoonful of dulce de leche on the flat side of one cookie. Top with second cookie, pressing gently to form a sandwich. Repeat with remaining filling and cookies. Store in an airtight container at room temperature.

Prep time:	15 min.
Cook time:	28 min.
Total time:	43 min.
Yield:	15 servings
Serving size:	1 sandwich cookie

TOTAL TIME 43 min.

TOTAL TIME 1 hr. 3 min.

Cinnamon Swirl Coffee Cake

Here's a reduced-sugar coffee cake that bursts with cinnamon flavor and features a mouthwatering crumb topping.

INGREDIENTS

1 1/2 c. evaporated cane juice sugar

3 large eggs

1 c. reduced-fat sour cream

3/4 c. Smart Balance Buttery Spread, softened

2 1/2 c. all purpose flour

1 tsp. baking soda

1 tsp. baking powder

1 tsp. vanilla extract

Cooking spray

INGREDIENTS Cinnamon Filling

2 tbsp. ground cinnamon

1/4 c. light brown sugar, lightly packed

DIRECTIONS

Adjust oven rack to upper-middle position and heat oven to 400 degrees. Lightly spray 9-inch round cake pan with cooking spray. In large mixing bowl or bowl of standing mixer, set on low, beat sugar and eggs until combined.

Add sour cream and Smart Balance spread and continue to beat until mixture is light and fluffy.

In separate medium-sized mixing bowl, combine flour, baking soda and baking powder, and stir until blended. Add flour mixture to liquid mixture, stirring or mixing on low speed just until combined. (Overbeating batter will create a tough, chewy cake.) Stir in vanilla extract.

In small bowl, combine and mix together brown sugar and cinnamon. Pour half of cake batter into prepared pan, then scatter brown sugar and cinnamon filling evenly over surface. Cover cinnamon filling with remaining batter. Bake for 8 minutes, then reduce oven heat to 350 degrees and bake for another 40 minutes. Allow cake to cool in pan for 20 minutes before removing from pan to cool. Keep on rack for 30 minutes, then cut and serve. Store remaining cake in refrigerator for up to three days.

Prep time:	15 min.
Cook time:	48 min.
Total time:	1 hr. 3 min.
Inactive:	50 min.
Yield:	10 servings
Serving size:	1 slice

NUTRITIONAL INFORMATION
Per Serving

Calories:	332
Total Fat:	13 g
Cholesterol:	54 mg
Sodium:	224 mg
Total Carbohydrates:	50 g
Fiber:	1 g
Sugars:	28.5 g
Protein:	5 g

White Chocolate Chip Cappuccino Cheesecake

NUTRITIONAL INFORMATION
Per Serving

Calories:	254
Total Fat:	14 g
Cholesterol:	81 m
Sodium:	404 mg
Total Carbohydrates:	25 g
Fiber:	1 g
Sugars:	15 g
Protein:	8 g

Not only does this cheesecake sounds decadent, it tastes decadent. We've found that Ghirardelli's white chocolate chips perfectly highlight the rich flavors of this cake.

INGREDIENTS

1 9" Graham Cracker Crust
   (see pg. 182 for crust recipe)

12-oz. reduced fat cream cheese
   (1 1/2 8 oz. bars), softened

1 c. nonfat ricotta cheese (3/4 lb.)

1/3 c. white chocolate chips

1/3 c. evaporated cane juice sugar

2 large egg yolks

1 large egg

1/4 c. sugar-free cappuccino mix

DIRECTIONS

Prepare Graham Cracker Crust (see pg. 182 for crust recipe) and have cooled crust ready for filling.

Adjust oven rack to upper-middle position and heat oven to 275 degrees.

In medium mixing bowl or bowl of standing mixer, combine all ingredients except white chocolate chips. Then, mix or beat on low until well combined and creamy. Stir in chips with spatula until blended into cheesecake mixture. Pour mixture into Graham Cracker Crust and bake for 30-45 minutes, or until very center of the cheesecake wobbles slightly (cake will continue cooking when removed from the oven).

Remove cheesecake from oven and cool on rack for 15 minutes, then chill in refrigerator for 4 hours or overnight.

Cut cheesecake into 10 slices for serving. Store remaining cheesecake in refrigerator, covered, for up to three days.

Prep time:	10 min.
Cook time:	45 min.
Total time:	55 min.
Yield:	10 servings
Serving size:	1 slice

TOTAL TIME 55 min.

TOTAL TIME 51 min.

Gingersnap Pumpkin Cheesecake

Here it is! Behold The Fresh Diet cheesecake recipe. We could never publish a cookbook and not include at least one of our famed and fabulous cheesecake recipes. It has earned its reputation as the king of desserts and for very good reason. Bear in mind that in order to make this famous cheesecake, it is important to use evaporated cane juice sugar. This is a more natural alternative to refined sugar because it does not undergo the same degree of processing. We have a feeling this might be the most "used" recipe in this whole book!

NUTRITIONAL INFORMATION
Per Serving

Calories:	282
Total Fat:	15 g
Cholesterol:	63 mg
Sodium:	260 mg
Total Carbohydrates:	30 g
Fiber:	1 g
Sugars:	17 g
Protein:	8 g

INGREDIENTS

12-oz. reduced fat cream cheese, softened

1 c. part-skim ricotta cheese

1/2 c. canned pumpkin puree

1/2 c. evaporated cane juice sugar

1 large egg yolk

1 large egg

1 tsp. ground ginger

1 prepared 9" gingersnap crust (see pg. 183 for crust recipe)

DIRECTIONS

Adjust oven rack to upper-middle position and heat oven to 275 degrees.

In large mixing bowl or bowl of standing mixer, combine cream cheese, ricotta, pumpkin, sugar, eggs and ground ginger and mix until well blended. Pour filling into cooled pie crust. Bake for 30-45 minutes until very center of cake wobbles slightly; cake will continue to cook and firm up once removed from oven. Cool on rack for 15 minutes, and then transfer to the refrigerator for 4 hours or overnight to completely cool before serving. When ready to serve, cut cheesecake into 10 portions. Store the remaining cheesecake in a covered container in refrigerator for up to three days.

Prep time:	6 min.
Cook time:	30-45 min.
Total time:	51 min.
Yield:	10 servings
Serving size:	1 slice

Key Lime Cheesecake

The Fresh Diet's key lime pie is a perennial favorite – creamy, flavorful, and featuring the classic Graham Cracker Crust. Best of all, it has fewer fat grams and less sugar than regular versions! To prepare, buy key limes more yellow (ripe) than green. When pressed for time, substitute with bottled key lime juice – we like the "Nellie and Joe's" brand – and a store-bought graham cracker crust.

NUTRITIONAL INFORMATION
Per Serving

Calories:	257
Total Fat:	14 g
Cholesterol:	82 mg
Sodium:	289 mg
Total Carbohydrates:	24.5 g
Fiber:	1 g
Sugars:	12 g
Protein:	8 g

INGREDIENTS

1 9" Graham Cracker Crust
  (see pg. 182 for crust recipe)

12-oz. reduced fat cream cheese
  (1 1/2 8-oz. bars), softened

1 c. skim ricotta cheese

1/3 c. fresh squeezed key lime
  juice (juice from 10 limes)

1/2 c. evaporated cane juice sugar

2 large egg yolks

1 large egg

DIRECTIONS

Prepare Graham Cracker Crust (recipe follows) and have cooled crust ready for filling.

Adjust oven rack to upper-middle position and heat oven to 275 degrees.

In large mixing bowl or bowl of standing mixer, combine all wet ingredients and mix until creamy and completely blended. Pour filling into cooled pie crust. Bake for 30-45 minutes until very center of cake wobbles slightly; cake will continue to cook and firm up once removed from oven. Cool on rack for 15 minutes, then chill in refrigerator for 4 hours or overnight.

When ready to serve, cut cheesecake into 10 portions. Store remaining cheesecake in covered container in refrigerator for up to three days.

Prep time:	6 min.
Cook time:	30-45 min.
Total time:	51 min.
Yield:	10 servings
Serving size:	1 slice

TOTAL TIME 51 min.

"They say, life is uncertain – eat dessert first." While we can't always condone such reckless behavior, when it comes to our famed cheesecake recipes, we might have to let this one slide. Perfection is in the details – that's why our crusts are not a one-size-fits-all option. We have added a special desserts addendum to make space for such details. This section will ensure your favorite cheesecakes are as perfect as you expect them to be. If there's one thing that can always be stretched out a little longer - it's dessert!

Graham Cracker Crust

NUTRITIONAL INFORMATION
Per Serving

Calories:	89
Total Fat:	5 g
Cholesterol:	0 mg
Sodium:	148 mg
Total Carbohydrates:	10 g
Fiber:	1 g
Sugars:	2 g
Protein:	1 g

INGREDIENTS

1 1/2 c. finely crushed graham crackers (about 18 graham crackers)

1/4 c. Smart Balance Buttery Spread, melted

DIRECTIONS

Adjust oven rack to upper-middle position, place cookie sheet on rack, and heat oven to 350 degrees. In medium mixing bowl, combine graham cracker crumbs and melted Smart Balance spread with rubber spatula until well mixed. Press crumbs into 9-inch pie plate, using your fingers or edge of a 1/4 cup measuring cup to make sure crumbs are firmly packed against bottom and side of plate.

Place pie plate on preheated cookie sheet, and bake crust for 7-10 minutes, or until lightly browned and fragrant. Remove from oven to cool (about 30 minutes) before filling.

Prep time:	5 min.
Cook time:	10 min.
Total time:	15 min.
Yield:	10 servings
Serving size:	1/10 crust

Gingersnap Crust

INGREDIENTS

1 1/2 c. ground gingersnap cookies
(about 28 cookies)

1/4 c. Smart Balance Buttery
Spread, melted

DIRECTIONS

Adjust oven rack to upper-middle position, place cookie sheet on rack, and heat oven to 350 degrees. In medium mixing bowl, combine gingersnap crumbs and melted Smart Balance spread with rubber spatula until evenly moistened. Press crumbs into 9-inch pie plate, using your fingers or bottom of a 1/4 cup measuring cup, making sure crumbs are firmly packed against bottom and side of plate. Place the pie plate on the preheated cookie sheet and bake crust, until deep golden brown and fragrant, 7-10 minutes. Remove from oven to cool (about 30 minutes) before filling.

Prep time:	5 min.
Cook time:	10 min.
Total time:	15 min.
Yield:	10 servings
Serving size:	1/10 crust

NUTRITIONAL INFORMATION
Per Serving

Calories:	116
Total Fat:	6 g
Cholesterol:	0 mg
Sodium:	120 mg
Total Carbohydrates:	15 g
Fiber:	0 g
Sugars:	7 g
Protein:	0 g

Acknowledgements

I would like to extend my sincere gratitude to all those whose contributions made the publishing of my very first cookbook a possibility.

I could not have completed this exciting project without the input and dedication of my team: Zalmi Duchman, Yuda Schlass, Ray Willig, Carlo Ricci, Carolina Ricci, José Bila Rodríguez, Theodora Kaloudis, Candy Tree, Brielle Batory and Rivky Grauman.

A special thank you must also be expressed to each and every one of the wonderful and devoted Executive Chefs and culinary teams. Not only did they tirelessly invest their time and efforts into this project, but they are the men and women that cook these great recipes for our clients to enjoy every day. Without all the employees at The Fresh Diet, we would not be witness to the growth and greatness of this company. I am proud to see what our collective effort has produced and built. The Fresh Diet is not just a business. It is a family and for many, an inspiration to better their health and their lives.

Without the love and unwavering support from my dear wife Rachel L. there is no way this book would have made it to print. Thank you! And thank you to each of the spouses of our Fresh Diet team. Without your encouragement, patience and tolerance for putting up with our demanding blackberries, this project would never have come to fruition!!

Each recipe in this book comes with a history of its own. For all of us at The Fresh Diet that have been a part of writing the story, the joy our clients and fans will receive from having our recipes in print is the best reward we can ask for!

It is my sincere hope that each meal is served and received with the same passion that went into creating them.

Bon Appétit!
Chef Yos